THE RIGHT JOKE
FOR THE
RIGHT OCCASION

Also available from Elliot Right Way Books

Public Speaker's Joke Book*
Wedding Speeches
Sample Social Speeches
Your Voice: How To Enrich It, And Develop It For Speaking,
   Acting And Everyday Conversation

By the same author

THE
RIGHT JOKE
FOR THE
RIGHT OCCASION

Kevin Goldstein-Jackson

RIGHT WAY

Typeset in 10/12pt Times by Letterpart Ltd., Reigate, Surrey.

Printed and bound in Great Britain by Cox & Wyman Ltd., Reading,
Berkshire.

The *Right Way* series is published by Elliot Right Way Books,
Brighton Road, Lower Kingswood, Tadworth, Surrey, KT20 6TD,
U.K. For information about our company and other books we
publish, visit our web site at www.right-way.co.uk

CONTENTS

DEDICATION

This book is dedicated to my wife, Mei Leng, for being so polite when I tell jokes – she covers her mouth when she yawns. She also knows all my jokes backwards – and frequently tells them that way. However, Mei Leng is the only woman I know who is like wine – she improves with age.

   The Right Joke For The Right Occasion is also dedicated to my two daughters, Sing Yu and Kimberley, who think I have a great sense of humour: what else could explain my style of clothes?

INTRODUCTION

As soon as people knew that I was writing another joke book, apart from almost unanimous cries of 'Oh, no!', they gave me jokes for inclusion in it – from friends (all two of them) to doctors, decorators and acquaintances.

Writing this book has certainly been good therapy to cheer myself up, and I hope it will do the same for you.

Some of the jokes you may well have heard of before, but I hope you will find a good number of them new, fresh and amusing; although some (particularly those based on puns) are intended to make you groan!

The jokes have been listed alphabetically under various subject headings, however sometimes it has been almost impossible to decide under which of several equally appropriate main headings a joke should appear.

If you are using this book as a source of humour for speeches, then please select the jokes most appropriate for your intended audience. For example, if certain people are told a joke with a double-meaning, they will fail to get either of them! And someone once defined tact as the ability to see others as they see themselves. Some jokes in this book are extremely old – but, then, nostalgia, too, is a thing of the past and yet many people still wallow happily in it. But it would be better to tell the older jokes to a younger audience which may not have heard them before.

It is also important to remember that the best speeches are short. Indeed, the best after-dinner speech consists of only five words. This is when someone other than yourself says, 'Please give me the bill.'

If you stumble or stutter while making a speech, say

something like: 'I knew I shouldn't have got these teeth by mail order.'

But I hope, after reading *The Right Joke For The Right Occasion*, you will not think of it in the same way as the girl who asked, 'Do you know what good clean fun is?', to which her boyfriend replied, 'No, what good is it?'

K.G-J.

DIRECTORY

If you are just reading the book for fun, skip the next few pages because the actual jokes don't start until page 13.

This section is for the person who has to make a speech, or who needs a joke on a particular subject. In the directory, the numbers shown are the *joke numbers*, not page numbers.

Remember that the secret of being a good teller of a joke lies as much in the way you tell it as in the joke itself. Be enthusiastic, watch the 'timing' of the 'punch line'. Never tell a joke which does not suit the company. In conversation, try to tell jokes which 'arise' from the subject being discussed. There are 985 jokes in the book, which should be enough to keep you going for several minutes!

A

ACCIDENTS

1. A man rushed into a pub in a rather agitated state. 'Does anyone here own a large black cat with a white collar?' he asked, somewhat nervously. There was no reply.

'Does anybody own a large black cat with a white collar?' asked the man again, raising his voice even higher above the general noise of the bar. But still no one answered his question.

'Oh dear,' muttered the man. 'I must have run over the vicar.'

2. Mr Smith was just crossing a road on a zebra crossing when a car came hurtling towards him and, although he tried to jump out of the way, the car still managed to hit his side causing him to be thrown to the ground. A loud cackling noise could be heard from the car as it sped away.

A policeman who had witnessed the accident rushed up to Mr Smith and asked: 'Did you see the driver? Or remember the car's registration number?'

'I didn't need to,' replied Mr Smith. 'It was my wife who did it.'

'How do you know?' asked the policeman.

'Simple!' replied Mr Smith. 'I'd recognise that hideous laugh anywhere.'

ACOUSTICS

3. The acoustics in the new theatre were so good the actors could hear every cough, whisper, crackle of sweet wrappers . . .

4. 'The acoustics in this theatre are fantastic.'
'Pardon?'

ACROBATS
5. I once knew two acrobats who fell head over heels in love.

ACTORS AND ACTRESSES
6. Timothy desperately wanted to be a famous actor and always believed in trying to 'live' any parts he was asked to play. When he was invited to audition for the part of Abraham Lincoln in a new play, Timothy read all about Lincoln. He researched Lincoln's background for weeks and then dressed to look exactly like him – black hat, black cloak, red sash and large black boots. After admiring himself in a mirror he set off for the audition. He didn't get the part – but on the way home he was assassinated.

7. A friend of mine knew his son was going to be an actor when he caught him opening the fridge and taking a bow when the little light came on.

8. When Herbert auditioned to play the part of one of the seven dwarfs the director told him that he'd made the short list.

9. Conceited actor: 'I've practised my art with diligence and talent for so many years now that there is nothing I cannot express simply by using my remarkably expressive face and without using mere words at all.'
    Long-suffering friend: 'Well, can you express in your face alone – and without using any words – the following: you are an eighteen-year-old man who is working down a coal mine and you have just heard – simultaneously – that you have won a fortune on the football pools and that your girlfriend, whom you love deeply, has been killed in a road accident by

your brother whom you also love dearly and your mother has run off with the milkman and the coal mine is about to cave in?'

10. The Hollywood film actress was getting married for the seventh time when the clergyman stumbled over the words of the ceremony.

'It's all right,' hissed the actress. 'Take it again from the top of page five.'

11. Andrea: 'Dorothy, I can't understand why you still live with that dreadful actor friend of yours. You admit that he was rude to you at the party last night, and he's not even a good actor!'

Dorothy: 'I know. But I can't bring myself to bite the ham that feeds me.'

12. The Hollywood actor's career was on the decline and he seemed to spend all his time 'testing' for parts he never got, or trying to be seen in the right places and at the right parties in the hope of impressing some film mogul. Yet throughout this lean period in his career he remained hopeful that an upturn would soon come and he would be on his way to stardom.

It was in this state of mind that he returned home from his latest 'test' and was appalled to discover that his apartment had been totally wrecked. Paintings had been pulled from the walls and jumped on; a fire extinguisher had been sprayed all over the furniture and curtains; all the bottles in the bar area had been smashed; and in the middle of it all sat his girlfriend with blood pouring from her nose and with all the signs of having been involved in a fierce struggle.

'Who was it?' demanded the actor. 'I'll kill him!'

'Darling,' sobbed the girlfriend. 'It . . . it was the drink that must have made him do it. He arrived here totally drunk and went berserk the minute I let him in. It . . . it was your agent.'

'Why didn't you say so as soon as I got here, instead of

sitting sobbing and bleeding like that?' demanded the actor.
'It must have been important for him to have come visiting
my apartment. Did he leave a message?'

13. Where do Hollywood actors and actresses pick their
noses? From an illustrated catalogue.

14. Theodore was so keen to get the part of Long John Silver
in a new film that he actually had his leg amputated. Unfortunately he was turned down as he'd had the wrong leg off.

15. I once knew the twenty-year-old daughter of a Hollywood film actress who kept getting depressed because she
didn't look as young as her mother.

16. Ever since the novice actress was told by the big movie
producer that she had a nice profile she's walked around
sideways.

17. The actress was so poor she lived on sponge pudding –
she sponged all the ingredients off her neighbours.

18. The ageing actor was trying to chat up the gorgeous
young girl.
    'Don't you recognise me?' he asked. She shook her head.
    'But I'm quite well known in the movies,' he continued.
    'Oh!' she said, her eyes lighting up. 'Where do you usually
sit?'

19. Two ageing film actresses were walking along when one
said: 'Do you know the best way to keep your youth?' The
other replied: 'Lock him in the bedroom.'

ADOLESCENCE
20. Adolescence is the period in life between puberty and
adultery.

ADULTS

21. Adults are people who have stopped growing at the ends but have started to grow in the middle.

22. The main difference between men and boys is that men's toys cost more money.

ADVERTISING

23. Worktex bras – the largest manufacturers of bras in the world. We have a hand in nine out of ten bras in Britain.

24. Midget seeks work – preferably as a stunt man.

25. Do you suffer from Dan Druff? Well, tell him to go away.

26. Little girl: 'Mummy, why are your hands so soft?'
Mother: 'Because I always use Pixie Solid for washing my dishes.'
Little girl: 'But why does it get your hands so soft?'
Mother: 'Because the money Pixie Solid pay me for this commercial enables me to buy an automatic dishwasher.'

27. For sale: two single beds and a worn carpet.

28. Lavatory cleaner wanted to work on chain gang. Could you do this job? Some people are a flushing success at it.

29. The tea manufacturers wanted a new advertising gimmick, so the senior creative man at their advertising agency decided to go to Rome to see if he could persuade the Pope to make a TV commercial.
The Pope gave the adman an audience and he made his request. 'We'll give you one hundred thousand pounds for a

ten second commercial. All you have to do is say: "Give us this day our daily tea".'

'I'm sorry,' replied the Pope, 'but I cannot do as you request.'

'Five hundred thousand,' offered the adman.

'I'm afraid not,' said the Pope, solemnly.

'All right. One million pounds. And that's our very last offer.'

But still the Pope refused to make the commercial and the adman left. On the way home the adman turned to his secretary and said: 'That's odd. I mean, the Pope refusing to do a commercial for tea. I wonder how much the bread people are giving him.'

ADVICE
30. John: 'I just don't know what to do. What would *you* do if you were in my shoes?'

Alan: 'Polish them.'

AGE
31. My girlfriend says she is 'pushing thirty' – but slapped my face when I asked her from which direction.

AIR STEWARDESS
32. The air stewardess was being interviewed by her boss. 'Tell me, what would you do if you found yourself in a shallow dive?'

Air stewardess: 'I'd drink up quickly and get out.'

ANGLING
33. Fred: 'The fishing today wasn't very good.'

Claude: 'But I thought you'd had fifty bites?'

Fred: 'So I did: one small fish and forty-nine mosquitoes.'

34. 1st fisherman: 'Is this a good river for fish?'

2nd fisherman: 'Yes. It's so good that none of them are willing to leave it.'

35. A man walked into a fishmonger's and asked to buy six trout.

'Certainly, sir!' said the fishmonger, selecting the trout. He was about to wrap them up when the man said: 'No! Please don't wrap them up yet. Can you just gently throw them to me one by one?'

'I can,' replied the fishmonger. 'But why?'

'Well,' responded the man. 'I've been fishing all night and haven't caught anything. At least if you throw those trout to me and I catch them I can honestly say when I get home that I've caught six trout.'

36. John: 'Why are you fishing under that bridge in the pouring rain?'

Brian: 'Because that's where the fish will go to shelter.'

37. 'I only went fly-fishing once. All I caught was a blue-bottle, a midge, and a pair of trousers.'

38. Does fishing result in net profits?

39. 'I'm never taking my sister fishing again,' sighed the small boy to his mother.

'Why not?' asked his mother. 'I know she's only two but the water isn't very deep and you can swim, so what's the problem?'

'She keeps eating all my maggots and worms.'

ANTI-SMOKING

40. The strong anti-smoker put a notice on the front door of his house stating: 'Abandon smoke all ye who enter here.'

ANTIQUES

41. Joan: 'Did you know I collect antiques?'
Erica: 'Yes – I've seen your husband.'

ARISTOCRACY

42. The party of American hog slaughterers had been touring London for several days, visiting all the sights and being accompanied by various tour guides.

'Tell me,' said one of the Americans to a tour guide, 'what's this "aristocracy" that you keep talking about. Who or what are they?'

'Aristocracy,' replied the guide, 'is a collective noun used to describe a group of people who owe their position to their parents who, in turn, owe it to theirs and so on. The position is such that they need not do much and generally lead a life of leisure without having to bother much about earning money by hard work.'

'Oh!' said the American who had asked the question. 'We have people like that in the USA too, only we call them tramps or hoboes.'

ARTIFICIAL INSEMINATION

43. All the farmers in the area were going over to artificial insemination for their herds – all, that is, except Walter Manglewurzel. Walter refused to have anything to do with such new-fangled ideas, but one day the vet decided to convince him of the advantages of artificial insemination for his herd of cows.

Well, Walter stopped harnessing his wife to the plough to listen to the vet, and he was pleased with what he heard and agreed to give the idea a try.

That afternoon, the vet returned and said: 'Did you put the bucket of hot water and a towel in the cowsheds like I asked?'

'Yes,' replied Walter. 'And there's a hook behind the door you can hang your trousers on.'

ASTROLOGERS

44. Two astrologers met each other in the street on a particularly cold and bitter day.

'Terrible winter we're having,' muttered one of the astrologers.

'Yes,' replied the other. 'It reminds me of the winter of 2057.'

AUTHORS

45. The famous author was boasting at a cocktail party: 'My last novel took three years to research and another year to write.'

Cocktail guest: 'What a waste of time. You could have bought one for about £5.'

46. His books are so bad they sell about as well as pork sausages in a synagogue.

B

BABIES

47. Sarah was walking along pushing her new baby in its pram when an old friend approached, looked into the pram and said: 'My, he's beautiful. He looks just like his father.'

'I know,' said Sarah. 'It's a pity he doesn't look more like my husband.'

48. Theobald: 'Darling, I know you're pregnant and that pregnant women often get strange cravings. But do you really have to eat so many old rubber tyres?'

Sandra: 'But I'm only trying to make sure we have a bouncing baby . . .'

49. Mr and Mrs O'Reilly had been trying for a son for many, many years and, after eleven daughters they were eventually rewarded with a son.

'Who does he look like?' asked a friend, visiting the maternity hospital to see Mrs O'Reilly.

'We don't know,' replied Mrs O'Reilly. 'We haven't looked at his face yet.'

50. The proud mother was showing off her new baby to her friend. 'Doesn't he look just like his father?' asked the mother.

'Yes,' replied the friend. 'But I shouldn't worry too much – he'll probably change for the better as he gets older.'

51. 'Ah,' said Mrs Bigginswhistle, peering into the pram at her friend's baby. 'He looks just like his father – lying there on his back clutching a bottle.'

52. The elderly aunt bent down and asked her three-year-old nephew: 'Can you tell me the name of your new baby sister?'

The little boy shook his head sadly and replied: 'I don't know what it is. I keep asking her but I can't understand a word she says.'

53. There were two babies in the pram. One baby turned to the other baby and said: 'Are you a little girl or a little boy?'

'I don't know,' was the giggled reply.

'I can tell,' said the first baby gleefully, and he dived beneath the bedclothes and then resurfaced. 'You're a girl and I'm a boy,' he announced proudly.

'That was clever,' said the baby girl. 'How could you tell?'

'Easy! You've got pink bootees and I've got blue ones.'

54. 'He's just like his father.'

'I know – bald, sleepy and uneducated.'

BANKING

55. Customer: 'And how do I stand for a £5,000 loan?'

Bank manager: 'You don't – you grovel.'

56. A young woman went into a bank and asked to withdraw some money.

'Can you identify yourself?' asked the bank clerk.

The young woman opened her handbag, took out a mirror, looked into it and said: 'Yes, it's me all right.'

57. Bank manager: 'And what sort of account would you like to open, Mr and Mrs Smith?'

Mrs Smith: 'A joint account: Mr Smith deposits and I draw out.'

BARBERS

58. Claude (looking at his barber's bill): 'What? Ten pounds just to cut my hair – but I'm nearly bald . . .'

Barber: 'I know, sir. My charge is one pound for cutting the hair and nine pounds for search fees.'

59. Barbers always seem to make cutting remarks.

60. As from midnight on Thursday, under a new pay award, barbers are to get fringe benefits.

61. The barber had rather dirty hands and, when his customer mentioned this, the barber replied: 'Well, no one has asked for a shampoo yet.'

BIBLE
62. Five-year-old Clarence: 'Grandma, why do you always read the Bible for several hours every evening?'

Grandmother: 'Because I'm swotting for my finals.'

63. It may interest many travellers to know that the railways system in Britain is mentioned in the Book of Genesis. It states that God created every creeping thing.

BIG GAME HUNTING
64. Simon: 'That's a lovely stuffed bear you've got in your hallway.'

Colonel Bloggis: 'Thank you. I shot that when I went to Alaska hunting with old Bill Bloggett-Sykes.'

Simon: 'What's the bear stuffed with?'

Colonel Bloggis: 'Old Bill Bloggett-Sykes.'

BIGAMY
65. Judge: 'You have been found not guilty of bigamy, so you can now be released and go home.'

Prisoner: 'Which home should I go to?'

BIRTHDAYS
66. Samantha: 'Do you know when Fred's birthday is?'
Sally: 'No. But I think it's sometime this year.'

67. I know a family that is so poor the parents couldn't afford to celebrate their son's eighteenth birthday until he was forty-nine.

68. My wife's best friend has just celebrated the twentieth anniversary of her twenty-ninth birthday.

BLOOD TEST
69. She's so stupid she spent hours in the library trying to study for her blood test.

BOASTING
70. John was always boasting. In fact, he was probably the biggest boaster in the world – and the most conceited. He was also incredibly fat and must have weighed at least twenty-five stone.

People were therefore surprised when John died and his coffin appeared to be extremely small.

'Is that really John in there?' asked one of the people at the funeral.

'Of course!' was the reply. 'When all the wind was let out of him he only needed a small coffin.'

BODY BUILDING
71. My aunt Gladys took up body building recently. She did it so well that now she's my uncle.

BOOKS
72. *How To Juggle With Empty Beer Bottles* by Beatrix.

73. *Twenty-six Letters In Order* by Alf A Bett.

74. *How To Tame Lions* by Claude Bottom.

75. *No Food* by M T Cupboard.

76. *Bull Fighting* by Matt A Dore.

77. *The Art of Striptease* by Eva Drawsoff.

78. *Outsize Clothes* by L E Fant.

79. *How To Improve Your Memory* by Ivor Gott.

80. *Home Haircutting* by Shaun Hedd.

81. *Pass The Sick Bags* by Eve Itt-Upp.

82. *Horse Riding Competitions* by Jim Karna.

83. *Panties Fall Down* by Lucy Lastic.

84. *Highwaymen Through the Ages* by Stan Dan D Liver.

85. *Not Quite The Truth* by Liza Lott.

86. *How To Make Solid Meals* by C Ment.

87. *How To Make An Igloo* by S K Mow.

88. *Quick Swim Across The English Channel* by Frances Near.

89. *Sleepless Nights Together* by Constance Norah.

90. *The Naughty Boy* by U R A Payne.

91. *Neck Exercises* by G Rarff.

92. *Uncertainty* by R U Shore.

93. *Deathly Cookery* by R Snick.

94. *Very Old Furniture* by Anne Teak.

95. *Want A Kiss?* by Miss L Toh.

96. *Singing Between Tenor And Bass* by Barry Tone.

97. *How To Grow Squashy Red Fruit* by Tom R Tow.

98. *How To Win* by Vic Tree.

99. *Carpet Fitting For All* by Walter Wall.

BOOKSHOP

100. Customer: 'I'd like to buy a novel, please.'

Bookshop assistant: 'Certainly, madam. Do you have the title or name of the author?'

Customer: 'Not really. I was hoping you could suggest something suitable that I could read.'

Bookshop assistant: 'No problem. Do you like light or heavy reading?'

Customer: 'It doesn't matter. I've left the car just outside the shop.'

BORROWING

101. There was a knock on the door. Mr Jones sighed and said to his wife: 'I bet it's that Bloggis fellow from next door wanting to borrow something else. He's already borrowed half the things in our house.'

'I know, dear,' replied Mrs Jones. 'But why do you have to

give in to him every time? Why not make some excuse so he can't borrow whatever he's come to borrow?'

'Good idea!' agreed Mr Jones and he went and opened the door to Bloggis.

'Good morning,' said Bloggis. 'I'm sorry to trouble you, but I wondered if you would be using your garden shears this afternoon?'

'I'm afraid I will,' responded Mr Jones. 'In fact, my wife and I will be spending the whole afternoon gardening.'

'That's what I thought,' said Mr Bloggis. 'Now I know you'll be too busy to use your golf clubs so perhaps you won't mind if I borrow them.'

BOSSES

102. Office junior: 'Please sir, can I have a day off next month?'

Boss: 'What for?'

Office junior: 'I'm getting married.'

Boss: 'But you don't earn very much; you look like a tramp; and you've no hope of ever rising above being an office junior. What sort of idiot would marry you?'

Office junior: 'Your daughter, sir.'

103. Sally: 'You have to admire the boss in my office.'

Samantha: 'Why?'

Sally: 'If you don't he demotes you to post-room messenger.'

104. Cyril: 'Do you still work for the same boss?'

Clifford: 'Yes – the wife and two kids.'

105. Employee: 'Please, sir, can I have a day off work next month?'

Boss: 'A day off next month! A day off next month! Whatever next! After all I've done for you over the past thirty years. Reasonable wages. You've never been ill so you've

always enjoyed your annual week's holiday. And after all
that you ask for a day off next month! Do I have to tolerate
such idiotic requests *every* thirty years?'

106. Everyone has a good word for our boss – but we have to
whisper it behind his back.

107. Office manager: 'Sir?'
   Boss: 'Yes? What is it now?'
   Office manager: 'Please can I have a day off next week to
do some late Christmas shopping with my wife and our six
kids?'
   Boss: 'Certainly not!'
   Office manager: 'I knew you'd be understanding, sir.
Thanks for getting me out of that terrible chore.'

108. Boss: 'Why are you late for work this morning?'
   Office manager's clerk: 'I'm sorry, sir. Normally I dream of
my favourite football team and wake up at 7 a.m. when the
game is over – but this morning they had to play extra time . . .'

109. My boss is like a lamb. Whenever anyone asks for a pay
rise or a day off he says: 'Baah!'

110. Employee: 'Sir, my wage packet this week was empty.'
   Boss: 'I know. They don't make money in small enough
denominations to pay you what you're worth.'

111. Office manager: 'Sir?'
   Boss: 'Yes, what is it?'
   Office manager: 'Sir, my wife said I should ask you for a
rise.'
   Boss: 'Hmm. I'll ask my wife tonight whether or not I
should give you one.'

112. The rather absent-minded boss was sitting in his London
office when the telephone rang. His secretary answered the

phone and said: 'It's a long-distance from New York.'

'I know it is,' said the boss, continuing to read his newspaper. 'In fact, I think it's about three and a half thousand miles.'

113. Angry employer: 'Why are you late again this morning?'

Young typist: 'I overslept.'

Angry employer: 'You mean, you sleep at home *as well*?'

114. At the company Board meeting the Chairman rose to make his speech. 'Who has been carrying on with my secretary?' he demanded.

This was met with silence. 'All right, then,' said the Chairman, 'put it this way – who has *not* been carrying on with my secretary?'

Again there was silence, and then one man said, self-consciously: 'Me, sir.'

'Right,' said the Chairman. '*You* sack her.'

115. Angry employer: 'You should have been here at nine o'clock.'

Late employee: 'Why, what happened?'

BUDGERIGARS

116. What do you call a constipated budgie? Chirrup of figs.

117. What do you call a nine foot budgie? Sir.

118. Where does a nine foot budgie sleep? Anywhere it wants to.

BUILDERS

119. Three builders were working on a building site, supposedly digging a trench. After a few hours the foreman came along and was surprised to find one of the men digging furiously while the other two were standing motionless, their shovels in the air, and claiming that they were both lamp posts. The foreman sacked the two men immediately and told them to go home. But the man in the trench also stopped work.

'It's all right,' said the foreman. 'I haven't fired you. You were working very well, so carry on.'

'How,' asked the man, 'do you expect me to work in the dark?'

120. Builder: 'I thought I recognised your daughter, sir. She was in the school that I was doing some work on. In the first year, I believe.'

Harassed man: 'And which year was she in when you had finished the work?'

121. Some workers were busy on a construction site next to a toy shop when suddenly they hit granite while digging a trench. They urgently needed some picks, but their base was about forty-five miles away and all workmen were being paid a bonus for speedy completion of the work. What could they do?

Fortunately, the toy shop had a large display in one of its windows in which life-size teddy bears appeared to be working in a coal mine. Each teddy bear clutched a pick in its paws.

The construction workers approached the toy shop owner and he agreed to let them borrow the picks for the rest of that day; the workmen promising to use their own picks the following day.

After working for about three hours very successfully, the workmen stopped for a brief lunch.

Unfortunately, when they returned, they found that all the picks had been stolen – to which a passer-by commented: 'Didn't you know that today's the day the teddy bears have their picks nicked?'

BURGERS
122. What do you say to a burger? How now? Ground cow.

BUS DRIVER
123. The only reason he became a bus driver was because he wanted to tell people where to get off.

BUSINESS CARDS
124. I know a man who hands out blank business cards – he wants to remain anonymous.

BUTCHER
125. Woman: 'I want a nice piece of bacon. And make it lean.'
    Butcher: 'Which way, madam?'

C

CAMELS

126. What do you call a camel with three humps? Humphrey.

127. Then there was the Arab who was so fat his camel had its hump underneath.

CANNIBALS

128. 'Do you like beans?'
  'Yes, very much.'
  'What sort do you like eating best?'
  'Human bein's.'

129. What do cannibals eat for breakfast? Buttered host.

130. I once met a cannibal who was constipated. I gave him some laxatives and he soon passed his cousin in the jungle.

131. The cannibal drank a lot of soup out of an enormous cooking pot, then turned to his friend, belched, and said: 'I've had a bellyful of your mother.'

132. 'Your wife makes lovely stew.'
  'I know – but I'll miss her.'

133. The cannibal came home to find his wife chopping up snakes and a very small man. 'Oh no!' he groaned. 'Not snake and pygmy pie again!'

134. As one cannibal said to the other, tasting the stew: 'It contains health-giving vitamin Bill Brown.'

CARPENTRY
135. How can you easily decide whether to use a screw or a nail when doing carpentry? Drive in a nail – if the wood splits, you should have used a screw.

136. It's easy for a carpenter to hammer in nails without hitting his fingers if he lets someone else hold the nail.

CARPET FITTING
137. Two men were fitting a wall-to-wall carpet in an elderly lady's house when they noticed a bump right in the middle of the carpet.

As they had finished fitting it, the workmen didn't really relish the thought of taking up the carpet again, especially as one of the workmen said: 'It must be that empty packet of cigarettes I was going to throw away.'

Thus, in order to get rid of the bump, the two workmen jumped up and down on it and it was soon flattened and the carpet now looked perfect.

Just then the lady came into the room and said: 'Excuse me, but I wondered if you had seen my budgie anywhere? It's hurt its wing and can't fly and so it just walks around on the floor.'

CARS
138. I once bought a car designed for five people: one had to drive while the other four pushed.

139. Janice: 'I think there's something wrong with the indicator lights on my car. Would you mind getting out of the car and calling out to me if they're OK or not?'

Janet: 'Certainly. Right. I'm ready. I'm looking at the indicator lights. Yes, they're working. No, they're not. Yes. No. Yes. No. Yes. No. Yes. No. Yes. No.'

140. I recently bought a baby car – it doesn't go anywhere without a rattle.

141. After close inspection of the circumstances leading to over a million car accidents around the world, investigators have proved conclusively that the part of a car most likely to cause an accident is the nut behind the wheel.

142. Derek: 'This car you sold me is useless.'
   Car dealer: 'What's wrong with it?'
   Derek: 'Within a week of me buying the thing, one of the doors fell off it, all the lights failed, the exhaust dropped off, the brakes failed, and the steering wheel came loose in my hands. I thought you said the car had only had one careful driver?'
   Car dealer: 'So I did. But the second owner wasn't quite so careful . . .'

143. One day Claude came home from work to find his wife painting one side of the car blue. She'd divided the car neatly in half and had already painted the other side bright yellow.
   'What on earth are you doing?' asked Claude.
   'Simple!' she replied. 'You know I've had so many accidents and I always get caught due to the statements of the witnesses in court. *Now*, if I have an accident, you watch them fight it out trying to decide what colour car caused the accident!'

144. Henry was trying to sell his battered old car for £1,500. His friend, Tom, said he would pay 10% less than the price Henry was asking for the car. But Henry was not very good at figures so he said he would think about Tom's offer. That evening, when he was in his usual bar, Henry asked the barmaid: 'If I offered you £1,500 less 10% what would you take off?'

The barmaid hesitated slightly, then replied: 'Everything except my ear-rings.'

145. I've got a two-tone car – black and rust.

CATS

146. The vet had just supervised the delivery of a litter of kittens to the old spinster's cat. 'I just don't know how it could have happened,' said the spinster. 'Tibbles is never allowed out and no other cats are ever allowed into the house.'

'But what about him?' asked the vet, pointing to a large tom cat sitting in an armchair.

'Oh, don't be silly,' replied the spinster. 'That's her brother.'

147. A friend of mine used to own the most inquisitive cat in the whole of China. It was a Peking Tom.

148. John: 'I have one of the most intelligent cats in the world.'

Simon: 'What does it do?'

John: 'Watch me pretend to shoot it. Bang! You're dead!'

Simon: 'But the cat didn't do anything – he's still just licking his paws.'

John: 'That's what I mean about him being intelligent: he knew he wasn't dead.'

CEMETERIES

149. Little Julian had been carefully examining all the tombstones in the cemetery and reading all the various inscriptions when he suddenly asked his father: 'Daddy, where do they bury all the horrible people?'

CHEMIST

150. Customer: 'Chemist, I'd like some poison for mice.'

Chemist: 'Have you tried Boots?'

Customer: 'I want to poison them – not kick them to death.'

CHILDREN

151. Mavis: 'My children are terrible. They climb all over everywhere and never give me a moment's peace. How do you keep so calm?'

Ethel: 'It's all due to the wonders of a play pen. I sit inside it and the kids can't get me!'

152. Mrs Smith: 'Have I told you about my children?'

Mrs Witherspoon: 'No. And I'm genuinely grateful to you for not telling me.'

153. Samantha: 'Mummy, Friday always comes before Thursday.'

Mother: 'I'm sorry, dear, but you are wrong.'

Samantha: 'I'm not. Friday always comes before Thursday in the dictionary!'

154. The children were happily playing in the garden when little Freda asked John if he wanted his palm read. When he said he did, she took out a pot of red paint she had been hiding behind her back and tipped it all over his hand.

155. Mother: 'Who are you writing to?'

Four-year-old daughter: 'Myself.'

Mother: 'What does the letter say?'

Four-year-old daughter: 'Don't be silly! How do I know? I haven't sent it and received it yet.'

156. Mother: 'Why did you put a newt in your sister's bed?'

Small son: 'Because I couldn't find a mouse.'

157. Father: 'What are you going to be when you've finished studying and passing all your exams?'
Son: 'Probably an old age pensioner.'

158. Small daughter: 'Mummy, how many more days is it before Christmas?'
Mother: 'Not many. Why do you ask?'
Small daughter: 'I just wondered if it's near enough for me to start being a good little girl.'

159. Mavis had told her daughter, three-year-old Fiona, to be on her best behaviour when she visited one of her aunts who was a stickler for good manners.
'Always say ''please'' and ''thank you'',' cautioned Mavis. 'And whatever you do, always be polite.'
Thus it was that at lunch when the aunt enquired of Fiona 'Can you manage with the meat? Or would you like me to cut it in small pieces for you? Fiona replied: 'No, thank you. I can manage on my own, thank you. We sometimes have meat as tough as this at home.'

160. 'Bernard!' screamed Bernard's mother. 'Why did you fall in that mud wearing your new trousers?'
'Because,' replied Bernard, 'there wasn't time to take them off.'

161. Four-year-old Diana was looking expectantly at her rather plump aunt as she sat at the dinner table.
'Why are you looking at me like that?' asked the aunt.
'Well,' replied Diana, 'I'm waiting for you to get your nosebag out.'
'My nosebag?'
'Yes. I heard Daddy tell Mummy last night that you ate like a horse.'

162. Mother: 'Now, let's see how clever you are, Joan. If I have six sweets and someone gives me another two sweets, how many sweets do I have?'

Very young daughter: 'I don't know, mummy. At nursery school we do all our sums with fingers or apples.'

163. Mother: 'Why are you crying?'
Sally: 'Because I fell over and hurt myself.'
Mother: 'When did you do that?'
Sally: 'About twenty minutes ago.'
Mother: 'But I've only just heard you crying – you haven't been crying for twenty minutes.'
Sally: 'I know. Earlier, I thought you'd gone out.'

164. Three-year-old Samantha had just been punished by her mother for telling lies. 'I never told lies when I was a little girl,' said Samantha's mother.
'Oh, mother,' sobbed little Samantha, 'so when did you start?'

165. Aunt: 'Now tell me, Juliet, what will you do when you are as big as your mother?'
Five-year-old Juliet: 'Go on a diet.'

166. It has been said that children brighten a home. I suppose that's because they never turn any of the lights off.

167. Very annoyed lady: 'I'll teach you to throw bricks at my greenhouse!'
Small boy: 'Thanks a lot, lady! When do the lessons start as I sure need them? My last five bricks missed.'

168. Terence: 'Mum, where do all the flies go in winter?'
Mother: 'Search me.'
Terence: 'No thanks. I believe you.'

169. Forgetful aunt: 'Hector, how old will you be next birthday?'

Hector: 'Six.'
Forgetful aunt: 'So on your last birthday how old were you?'
Hector: 'Four.'
Forgetful aunt: 'Four? How can that be if you will be six on your next birthday?'
Hector: 'Easy! I'm five today.'

170. My children have so many things in their rooms – TV, CD player, books, games – that, when they are naughty, as a punishment I have to send them to *my* room.

171. Mrs Gruntleburger was rather surprised at how well behaved her little niece appeared to be.

'You're very quiet,' she said. 'Why are you so well behaved and quiet?'

The little niece replied: 'Because mummy has promised me I can have a new teddy bear if I don't say anything about your enormous nose and funny ears.'

172. Amelia didn't know what to do with her seven-year-old son, Reginald. Every time a visitor came to the house or he saw someone he didn't know he would race towards them and bite them on the knee. Then he would cling to their legs and refuse to let go.

In desperation, Amelia took Reginald to a child psychologist and, on seeing the psychologist, Reginald rushed towards him, bit his knee and then clung to the man's legs.

The child psychologist looked down at Reginald, then bent and whispered something in the boy's ear. Immediately, Reginald let go of the man's legs and ran back to his mother.

'He's cured!' cried Amelia. 'What did you say to him?'

The child psychologist smiled and said: 'I told him that if he didn't let go of my legs I'd smash his stupid face in.'

173. 'Mummy,' said five-year-old Brian, 'I've been very good and filled the salt cellar like you asked me to, but it's taken a very long time.'

'Why is that?'

'Because it was very difficult getting the salt in through that tiny hole in the top.'

174. 'Auntie,' said five-year-old Mandy. 'I don't think mummy knows how to bring up children properly. Can you speak to her?'

'Why? What has she done?' asked Mandy's aunt.

'I'm sure she doesn't know anything about raising children. She always sends me to bed when I don't feel sleepy and wakes me up when I'm still tired.'

175. Health visitor: 'Why do you keep having more children? You've already got nine — and now you're pregnant again!'

Woman: 'I know. But you wouldn't want the youngest child to keep getting spoiled, would you?'

176. 'Mummy, Mummy! Look at me!' shouted six-year-old Derek while hanging twenty feet above the ground from a branch of a tree.

'Derek!' shouted his mother in reply. 'If you fall and break your legs don't come running to me!'

177. Mother: 'Today you have a choice for dinner. You either eat it – or you leave it.'

178. John: 'Mummy, Barry has just broken a pane of glass in the greenhouse.'

Mother: 'How did he do that?'

John: 'I threw my cricket bat at him and he ducked.'

179. Four-year-old Claire was a difficult child and didn't seem to want to eat anything other than chocolates and cake and biscuits.

'Come on,' urged her mother. 'Eat your dinner.'

'I don't want it,' said Claire.

'But there are millions of children in Africa who would be glad of a meal like that.'

'Then name one of them,' said Claire, triumphantly.

CHRISTENING
180. Rodney: 'Why are you so pleased your mother christened you "John"?'

John: 'Because that's what everyone calls me.'

CHURCH
181. Sarah is a regular church-goer – she goes every Christmas.

182. 'Next week,' said the vicar, 'my sermon will be entirely about truthfulness and I think it is especially important that on getting home from church today – or at least sometime during the week – that you read the twenty-ninth chapter of Leviticus.'

The following week the vicar started his sermon: 'Last week I said that my sermon this week would be about truthfulness and I asked you all to read the twenty-ninth chapter of Leviticus. Now, can all those who did this please raise their right hands.'

Almost the entire congregation raised their right hands.

'Just as I suspected!' said the vicar. 'And that is why my sermon today is about truthfulness. You could not possibly have read the twenty-ninth chapter of Leviticus. Leviticus only has twenty-seven chapters.'

183. Four-year-old James came home from a visit to the church with his aunt and told his mother: 'I was very good and didn't give in to temptation. When they brought round a huge plate with money on it I said I didn't want it.'

184. Candida was eighty years old and one day she went to confession and said: 'Father, I have sinned. I have committed adultery with a seventeen year old gardener.'

'When was this?' asked the priest.

'Fifty years ago – but I just felt like recalling pleasant experiences this week.'

185. It was the little English girl's first visit to a church in the USA.

The clergyman was an extremely energetic preacher and during his sermon he stood in the pulpit and gestured wildly with his hands, shouted and wailed at his congregation, cajoled them, thumped the sides of the pulpit with his fists to emphasise certain points, and his facial expressions ranged from rage to kindness but all with extreme emotive passion.

As the clergyman stamped his feet and banged on his pulpit again, the little girl turned to her mother and whispered: 'I hope they keep him locked up in that little box – I wouldn't like to be near him if he gets out.'

CINEMA

186. I once went to a cinema and watched a mad, passionate scene that lasted for almost half an hour – then I had to stop looking at the back row and watch the film.

187. Young girl in a cinema: 'Take your hand off my knee! No, not you, *you!*'

188. The man in the front seat of the cinema was making groaning noises very loudly during a tender love scene on the screen.

'Shut up!' hissed the audience around him, but still the man continued making horrible noises.

Eventually, the manager was called and he marched down the aisle until he came to the noisy man. 'Get up!' demanded the manager.

'Ooooooh! Aaaaaaaargh!' shouted the man, in reply.

'Where are you from?' asked the manager.

'F . . . Fr . . .' groaned the man '. . . from th . . . the balcony.'

189. Dracula films are fangtastic.

190. The young girl was complaining to one of her friends. 'It was terrible! I had to change my seat five times at the cinema last night.'

'Why?' asked the friend. 'Did some chap bother you?'

'Yes – eventually.'

CIVIL SERVICE

191. When James graduated from Oxford he applied for a position in the Civil Service. At his selection interview he was asked: 'What can you do well?'

James thought for a moment and then replied: 'Nothing.'

'Good!' cried the selection panel in unison. 'You're just the sort of chap we want – and we won't even have to break you in!'

CLEANERS

192. Theodora had found it difficult to find a suitable cleaner for her luxury apartment and she was delighted when a domestic services agency sent her someone who, at long last, looked ideal.

Theodora gestured to some paintings hanging on one of the walls. 'These paintings have to be treated with the utmost care as they are old masters.'

'Really?' said the cleaner. 'I didn't realise you had been married so many times.'

CLERGYMAN

193. A rather stone-faced and cold, celibate clergyman died and, soon after, one of his best friends also passed away.

On arriving in the 'other place' the clergyman's friend was surprised to see the clergyman with two beautiful blonde ladies sitting on his knee, and a gorgeous black-haired lady was stroking his shoulders and all three were clearly trying to seduce him.

'I see you're being well treated,' said the friend. 'I didn't realise Heaven was going to be so good.'

'I'm not enjoying myself,' replied the clergyman with a sour look. 'And this isn't Heaven. We're all in Hell – and I'm these three ladies' punishment.'

194. 'My Catholic priest knows more than your Methodist minister,' said ten-year-old Nathan.

'Of course he does,' replied David. 'You have to tell him everything.'

195. Vicar: 'Now tell me, Freda, how many times a day do you say your prayers?'

Four-year-old Freda: 'Once, sir. At night.'

Vicar: 'But don't you say any prayers at all during the day?'

Four-year-old Freda: 'No, sir. I'm only frightened at night.'

CLOAKROOM ATTENDANT
196. The theatre's cloakroom attendant was obviously very new to her job, and the man watched in silent amusement while she struggled to find his coat. She knocked clothes off their hangers and became more and more flustered when she could not trace the man's coat.

After nearly fifteen minutes of searching, a long queue had built up behind the man and his air of quiet amusement had given way to anger. Eventually he muttered: 'Don't bother to continue looking for my coat – I'll go without it. Perhaps if I come back tomorrow you might have found it. Although that seems most unlikely as you're the most incompetent person I've ever had the misfortune to meet!'

As he began to make his way out of the theatre the cloak-room attendant called: 'You mean old man! What about my tip?'

CLOCKS

197. The German could not get his clock to work properly. No matter what he did with it – shake it, take the back off it, blow on it – the clock insisted on only going 'tick'. Finally, his patience at an end, the German held up the clock in front of him and hissed: 'Ve haf vays of making you tock.'

198. Tom's grandfather collected clocks. By the time he died he had 2,378 different clocks and it's been taking Tom ages to wind up his grandfather's estate.

199. Albert: 'I threw my alarm clock away this morning.'
  John: 'Why?'
  Albert: 'It kept going off when I was asleep.'

CLOTHES

200. 'That's a nice suit you're wearing – who went for the fitting?'

201. I always dress to please my husband – I make each dress last at least ten years.

202. I've just bought a suit that fits me like a glove – four trouser legs and one sleeve.

203. Cyril's wife had moaned at him: 'I'm fed up with all these cheap coats you make me wear – all synthetic materials and horrible. Why can't you buy me a nice animal skin one instead?' So Cyril went and bought her a donkey jacket.

204. My husband wears clothes that will never go out of style – they'll always look ridiculous.

205. Sally: 'I always know what to do to cheer myself up. Whenever I'm down in the dumps I get myself some new clothes.'

Samantha: 'So that explains it! I always wondered where you got such unusual clothes.'

206. 'This pair of shoes you sold me last week is ridiculous! One of them has a heel at least two inches shorter than the other. What do you expect me to do?'

'Limp.'

COMPETITION

207. John: 'Why are you so sad? You've just won first prize with your raffle ticket and got yourself a brand new car.'

Brian: 'I know. But I bought two tickets and the other one didn't win anything so I wasted my money on it.'

CONVERSATIONS

208. Caller: 'Hello? Is that the Wigglesby residence?'

Fred Bloggis: 'No. I'm afraid it isn't.'

Caller: 'Oh! I must have dialled the wrong number. I'm sorry to have troubled you.'

Fred Bloggis: 'No trouble at all. The phone was ringing anyway.'

209. 'Well, how do you find yourself these cold, winter mornings?'

'Oh, I just throw back the blankets and there I am.'

210. 'Will the band play anything I request?'

'Certainly, sir.'

'Then tell them to play dominoes.'

211. 'What do virgins eat for breakfast?'
'I don't know.'
'Huh! Just as I thought.'

212. 'Mummy, there's a man with a bill at the door.'
'Don't be silly, dear. It must be a duck with a hat on.'

213. Man: 'My sister married an Irishman.'
Friend: 'Oh, really?'
Man: 'No, O'Reilly.'

214. 'Do you come here often?'
'I'm your wife, stupid!'

215. 'I didn't come here to be insulted.'
'Why – where do you normally go?'

216. 'Did he have a weakness for ladies?'
'No – a great strength.'

217. 'I say! Look over there – isn't that Hortense?'
'No – she looks quite relaxed to me.'

218. 'Understand you buried your wife last week?'
'Had to . . . dead, you know.'

219. 'What are you doing in the cellar, children?'
'Making love.'
'That's nice, dears. Don't fight.'

220. 'Do you smoke after making love?'
'I don't know, I've never looked.'

221. 'Excuse me, can you tell me the time?'
'I'm sorry, but I'm a stranger here myself.'

222. 'Why are you so angry?'
'Because it's all the rage.'

223. 'My mother made me a homosexual.'
'If I sent her the wool, would she make me one too?'

COURTROOM
224. The scene is a law court. The prosecution counsel faces the female witness and rasps: 'Is it true you committed adultery on the 18th of June in a snowstorm while riding on the roof of an automobile travelling at ninety miles an hour through Slough with a one-legged dwarf waving a Union Jack?'

The young woman in the witness box looked straight at the prosecuting counsel and said, calmly: 'What was the date again?'

225. A dry cleaner was excused jury service yesterday because he claimed his business was very pressing.

226. Judge: 'Did you sleep with this woman?'
Man in witness box: 'No, your honour, not a wink.'

227. Policeman in witness box: 'This woman came up to me when I was in plain clothes and tried to pass off this five pound note, m'lud.'
Judge: 'Counterfeit?'
Policeman in witness box: 'Yes, m'lud, she had two.'

228. The judge found the blacksmith guilty of forging.

229. The judge gave the man who stole a calendar twelve months.

230. Judge: 'How do you plead? Guilty or not guilty?'
Prisoner: 'How do I know, your honour? I haven't heard the evidence yet.'

231. When the prisoner appeared in court accused of stealing five skunks from the zoo the cry soon went up: 'Odour in court!'

232. In the divorce court the judge frowned and said: 'So, Miss Brown, you admit that you stayed in a hotel with this man?'

Woman: 'Yes, I do. But I couldn't help it. He deceived me.'

Judge: 'Really? How?'

Woman: 'Well, he told the reception clerk I was his wife.'

COWBOYS

233. The Lone Ranger and Tonto were riding along one morning when suddenly they saw five hundred Sioux chasing up behind them. Galloping ahead as fast as they could they were astonished to find another five hundred Indians – this time Apaches – racing towards them from the front, all dressed in war paint and giving excited war whoops.

The Lone Ranger slowed his horse to a gentle trot and turned to Tonto and said: 'Well, old friend, it looks as if this is going to be the finish for both of us.'

Tonto shook his head sadly, and said: 'What do you mean *both* of us – White Man?'

234. Two men in a saloon were playing cards. One of them thumped the table happily with his fist and cried: 'I win!'

'What have you got?' asked the other cowboy.

'Four aces.'

'I'm afraid you don't win.'

'That's almost impossible,' declared the first man. 'What cards have you got?'

'Two nines and a loaded gun.'

'Oh,' said the first man. 'You win. But how come you're so lucky?'

235. It was in the days of the old Wild West and the sheriff was hunting for a man who was dressed entirely in tissue paper. It seems he was wanted for rustling.

236. Hank: 'They call this here ranch the Lone Circle Triple Diamond Lazy Q Bar T Homestead.'
Clara: 'How many head of cattle do you have?'
Hank: 'Two. None of the rest survived the branding.'

237. 'Who painted my horse blue?' yelled the angry cowboy, entering the saloon.
Everyone was silent, and then a massive cowboy stood up and admitted to having done the deed. As he looked up at the huge man towering over him the newcomer said softly: 'Oh! I only wanted to know when you're going to give it a second coat.'

COWS
238. Farmer: 'Stop it! Stop it! Why are you beating the feet of the cows like that and making them jump up and down?'
Brian: 'I'm trying to make a milk shake.'

239. The first time the little girl from the big city ever saw a cow she thought it was a bull that had swallowed a glove.

CRAP GAME
240. My husband is so stupid he thinks a crap game is where people take bets on who can throw dried cow droppings the farthest.

CROCODILE
241. What do you call a crocodile at the North Pole? Lost.

D

DANCING

242. 'I had to give up tap dancing.'
  'Why?'
  'I kept falling in the sink.'

243. The go-go dancer was so bad everyone said she was more like a gone-gone dancer.

DANGER

244. In dangerous situations I always keep a cool head – usually on the top shelf of the larder.

DATING

245. Jonathan was a successful businessman but he'd been so busy making money he'd never had time to find himself a proper girlfriend so one day he wrote off to a computer dating agency that promised him the perfect match.

He was delighted to receive the name of a girl who lived nearby and decided to phone her to arrange their first meeting.

'And I'll meet you in the lounge area of the Golden Fleece restaurant – but how will I recognise you?' he asked.

'Well, I'll be wearing my scarlet dress, with scarlet shoes and a round scarlet hat.'

'Oh!' cried Jonathan happily, 'I always knew you'd be one in vermilion!'

DEFINITIONS

246. Bacteria: the back entrance to a cafeteria.

247. Blunderbuss: a coach load of spinsters on their way to a maternity hospital.

248. Buoyant: male equivalent of gallant.

249. Catacomb: a comb for a cat.

250. Cloak: mating call of a Chinese frog.

251. Countdown: something they do in an eiderdown factory.

252. Dogma: the mother of puppies.

253. Eunuch: man cut out to be a bachelor.

254. Filing cabinet: a useful container where things can be lost alphabetically.

255. Ghoulash: a cremated ghost.

256. Kipper: a fish that sleeps a lot.

257. Mistress: something between a mister and a mattress.

258. Mushroom: place where Eskimos train their dogs.

259. Myth: unmarried female with a lisp.

260. Octopus: an eight-sided cat.

261. Polysyllables: the language of parrots.

262. Signature tune: song of a young swan (cygnet).

263. Ultimate: the last person to marry.

264. Vice versa: dirty poems.

DENTIST
265. Man: 'Give it to me straight – how am I?'

Dentist: 'Well, sir your teeth are all right – but I'm afraid your gums will have to come out.'

DIETING
266. At a recent lecture entitled 'How To Lose Weight Easily', Mrs Emily Plum told the amazing story of how she lost over eighteen pounds in five minutes. Said this remarkable lady: 'I just cut off a leg.'

267. When my husband went on a diet for two weeks all he lost was a fortnight.

DISCOS
268. It was the first time forty-eight-year-old Avis Wigglesworth had been to a disco and she had only gone as a special favour to her daughter who had entered a dance contest at the disco and said she needed every supporter in the audience she could get.

As Avis looked around the room she muttered to the person standing next to her: 'This is an amazing place. And the people are even more incredible. Just look at that girl over there – dyed green hair, yellow jeans that fit like snakeskin, ten inch heels on her shoes . . .'

'That,' said the person next to Avis, 'is not a girl. That is my son.'

'Oh, I'm sorry,' said Avis, blushing with embarrassment. 'I didn't know you were his father.'

'I'm not,' was the reply. 'I'm his mother.'

DOCTOR, DOCTOR!

269. 'Doctor, I'm worried about my wife. She thinks she's a bird.'

'Well, you had better bring her in to see me.'

'I can't. She's just flown south for winter.'

270. The medical student was accompanying one of the consultants on his hospital rounds. Time after time, the student made a completely wrong diagnosis.

'Have you ever thought about taking up a different career?' asked the consultant. 'One where you would not be fired for frequent mis-diagnoses – such as a government economist?'

271. 'Doctor, doctor! I've just swallowed a spoon.'

'Sit down and don't stir.'

272. 'Doctor, doctor! I'm terribly worried. I keep seeing pink striped crocodiles every time I try to get to sleep.'

'Have you seen a psychiatrist?'

'No – only pink striped crocodiles.'

273. Patient: 'Doctor, how can I live to be a hundred?'

Doctor: 'Well, I suggest you give up eating rich food and going out with women.'

Patient: 'And then will I live to be a hundred?'

Doctor: 'No – but it will seem like it.'

274. Patient: 'Doctor, my hair keeps falling out. Have you got anything to keep it in?'

Doctor: 'What about a cardboard box?'

275. Patient: 'I feel like a very old sock.'

Doctor: 'Well, I'll be darned!'

276. Doctor: 'Nurse! Did you take this patient's temperature?'

Nurse: 'Why, doctor? Is it missing?'

277. Patient: 'Doctor! I don't know what's wrong with me but my body feels like jelly and my head has turned all yellow – as yellow as custard.'

Doctor: 'I think you must be a trifle ill.'

278. Patient: 'Doctor, I feel like a pack of cards.'

Doctor: 'Just sit down and I'll deal with you in a minute.'

279. Receptionist: 'Dr Wynazonski is waiting for you.'

Patient: 'Which doctor?'

Receptionist: 'Oh, no, he's fully qualified.'

280. Patient: 'Doctor, I think I have an inferiority complex.'

Doctor: 'Don't be silly. You really are inferior.'

281. Doctor: 'Now, you see that bottle on the table over there?'

Male patient: 'Yes, doctor.'

Doctor: 'Well, I want you to give me a sample of urine in it.'

Male patient (amazed): 'You expect me to do it from here? But what if some falls on the carpet before reaching that far?'

282. The only reason doctors wear masks when they perform operations is so that no one can recognise them if anything goes wrong.

283. Doctor: 'Now, tell me, have you ever had any trouble with diarrhoea?'

Patient: 'Only once.'

Doctor: 'And when was that?'

Patient: 'When I was at school and was asked to spell it.'

284. Patient: 'Doctor, I keep thinking I'm a dwarf who likes backing race horses.'

Doctor: 'There! Didn't I say those pills would make you feel like you were a little better!'

285. Patient: 'Doctor, my wooden leg keeps giving me the most awful pain.'

Doctor: 'Don't be ridiculous! How can a wooden leg give you pain?'

Patient: 'My wife keeps hitting me on the head with it.'

286. Patient: 'I've got bananas growing out of my ears.'

Doctor: 'Good gracious! How did that happen?'

Patient: 'I beg your pardon?'

287. Patient: 'Doctor, doctor! I think I'm becoming invisible.'

Doctor: 'Who said that?'

288. Patient: 'Doctor, do you think that I will live until I'm a hundred?'

Doctor: 'Do you smoke or drink?'

Patient: 'No, doctor, never.'

Doctor: 'Do you drive fast cars, gamble, or play around with women?'

Patient: 'Certainly not!'

Doctor: 'Then what do you want to live until a hundred for?'

289. Patient: 'Doctor, doctor! You've got to help me. I've just swallowed half a tin of gold paint.'

Doctor: 'How do you feel?'

Patient: 'Gilty.'

290. Patient: 'Doctor, you've already said that the operation is very risky. What are my chances of survival?'

Doctor: 'Excellent! The odds against success are 99 to 1, but the surgeon who will be performing the operation on you is looking forward to it as you will be his hundredth patient and so you must be a success after all the others!'

291. Patient: 'And when my right arm is quite better, will I be able to play the trumpet?'

Doctor: 'Most certainly – you should be able to play it with ease.'

Patient: 'That's wonderful – I could never play it before.'

292. The doctor had just finished examining the very attractive young girl.

Doctor: 'Have you been going out with men, Miss Jones?'

Miss Jones: 'Oh, no, doctor, never!'

Doctor: 'Are you quite sure? Bearing in mind that I've now examined the sample you sent, do you still say you've never had anything to do with men?'

Miss Jones: 'Quite sure, doctor. Can I go now?'

Doctor. 'No.'

Miss Jones. 'But why not?'

Doctor: 'Because, Miss Jones, I'm awaiting the arrival of the Three Wise Men.'

293. Patient: 'And if I take these little green pills exactly as you suggested, will I get better?'

Doctor: 'Well, let's put it this way – none of my patients has ever come back for more of those pills.'

294. Patient: 'Doctor, doctor! I keep thinking I'm a clock.'

Doctor: 'That sounds rather alarming! But don't you worry – we'll soon find out what makes you tick.'

295. Patient: 'Doctor, I think I'm turning into a Chihuahua.'

Doctor: 'Why not sit down and tell me all about it?'

Patient: 'I can't. Dogs aren't allowed on the furniture.'

296. A trade union leader went to his doctor for help in getting to sleep. The doctor was reluctant to put the union leader on sleeping pills until other remedies had been tried and so he asked the man to lie quite still in bed at night and count sheep.

The trade union leader did this, but by the time he'd counted the twenty-seventh sheep they'd all gone on strike for shorter hours and lower fences.

297. A man walked into the doctor's surgery and said: 'Can you help me? I've suddenly got a funny feeling in my head – it's all hot and I can't see. I also walk with a limp as one leg seems shorter than the other.'

The doctor looked at him thoughtfully for a moment and then said: 'It might help if you took your left boot off your head and put it back on your foot.'

298. 'Doctor, doctor! I think I've got measles.'

'That's a rash thing to say.'

299. The doctor looked at the man in front of him who was only about five feet tall, but who was also probably five feet wide: totally obese!

'Hmm,' said the doctor, producing two enormous pills which weighed about ten kilos each.

'But I can't possibly swallow huge pills like that,' protested the obese man.

'Who said you had to swallow them?' asked the doctor. 'All you've got to do is pick them up and raise them over your head and keep putting them down and picking them up for an hour a day.'

300. A doctor and his wife were sitting in deck chairs on the beach when a beautiful young girl in a very brief bikini jogged towards them. As she came to the doctor she waved at him and said, in a huskily sexy voice: 'Hi, there!' before continuing on her way.

'Who was that?' demanded the doctor's wife.

'Oh, just someone I met professionally,' replied the doctor.

'Oh, yes!' snorted the wife. 'Whose profession? Yours or hers?'

301. Patient: 'Doctor, people keep ignoring me.'

Doctor: 'Next patient, please!'

302. The man staggered into the doctor's surgery. He had three knives protruding out of his back, his head was bleeding from a gunshot wound, and his legs had been badly beaten by a hockey stick.

The doctor's receptionist looked up at this pitiful sight and said: 'Do you have an appointment?'

303. Patient: 'Doctor, doctor! I'm a kleptomaniac.'
Doctor: 'Are you taking anything for it?'

304. Doctor: 'Have you ever had your eyes checked?'
Patient: 'No, doctor. They've always been brown.'

305. Patient: 'Doctor, I keep thinking I'm a pair of curtains.'
Doctor: 'Well, pull yourself together.'

306. Patient: 'Doctor! Can you give me anything to stop me from sleepwalking?'
Doctor: 'Here's a box of a special item that should solve your problem. After you've got in bed for the night, sprinkle the contents of the box on the floor around your bed.'
Patient: 'What's in the box, doctor? Is it a powder that gives off a special odour?'
Doctor: 'No. Inside the box are drawing pins.'

307. Patient: 'Doctor, are these pills addictive?'
Doctor: 'Of course not! I've been taking them for years.'

308. Patient: 'Doctor, doctor! I keep talking to myself.'
Doctor: 'That's nothing to worry about. Lots of people mutter to themselves.'
Patient: 'But I'm a life assurance salesman and I keep selling myself policies I don't want.'

309. Doctor: 'I'm afraid your records haven't reached me yet from your previous doctor and my scales have just been broken by an enormously fat lady patient of mine. But can you tell me your average weight?'

Patient: 'I'm sorry, I don't know.'

Doctor: 'Do you know the most you have weighed?'

Patient: 'I think it was twelve stone nine pounds.'

Doctor: 'And what was the least you've weighed?'

Patient: 'I think that was about seven pounds three ounces.'

310. Doctor: 'Do you snore at night?'

Patient: 'Only when I'm asleep.'

311. Patient: 'Doctor, doctor! What do I need for ingrowing toenails?'

Doctor: 'Ingrowing toes.'

312. 'Doctor, how is little Fred who swallowed all the fire-crackers?'

'I don't know. We haven't had the final report.'

313. Doctor's wife: 'Why are you looking so worried, dear?'

Doctor: 'I think I've at last cured that Smith fellow.'

Doctor's wife: 'So why are you so worried?'

Doctor: 'I've given him so many pills and potions I can't work out which one worked.'

314. Patient: 'Doctor! I keep feeling I'm a bell.'

Doctor: 'Well, give me a ring when you're feeling a bit better.'

315. Doctor: 'I want you to take these two pills.'

Patient: 'What are they for?'

Doctor: 'The pink pill is to make you get some sleep – and you take the green pill if you don't wake up.'

316. The doctor told the portly gentleman: 'Now, take these pills and do more exercise and I hope to see nine-tenths of you back here next month.'

317. Nurse: 'Doctor, why are you trying to write that prescription with a thermometer?'

Absent-minded doctor: 'Drat! some silly bum must have my biro!'

318. Patient: 'Doctor! I feel as if I'm at death's door.'

Doctor: 'Don't worry. I'll soon pull you through.'

319. Worried patient: 'Doctor, I'm very worried. I'm still suffering from exhaustion and fatigue when I come home from work every evening.'

Doctor: 'Oh, that's nothing to worry about. Just have a few drinks before your dinner – that will soon wake you up.'

Patient: 'Thanks very much, doctor! But when I consulted you before, you told me to cut out drinking alcohol completely.

Doctor: 'Yes, so I did. But that was last week, old chap – and medical science has progressed enormously since then.'

320. Grandma was nearly ninety years of age when she won £1,000,000 on the football pools. Her family were extremely worried about her heart and feared that news of her large win would come as too much of a shock for her.

'I think we had better call in the doctor to tell her the news,' suggested the eldest son.

The doctor soon arrived and the situation was explained to him.

'Now, you don't have to worry about anything,' said the doctor. 'I am fully trained in such delicate matters and I feel sure I can break this news to her gently. I assure you, there is absolutely no need for you to fear for her health. Everything will be quite safe if left to me.'

The doctor went in to see the old lady and gradually brought the conversation around to football pools.

'Tell me,' said the doctor, 'what would you do if you had a

large win on the pools – say one million pounds?'

'Why, replied the old lady, 'I'd give half of it to you, of course.'

The doctor fell down dead with shock.

321. Patient: 'Doctor, sorry to trouble you again, but what can you give me for flat feet?'

Doctor: 'What about a bicycle pump?'

322. Student doctor: 'Please sir, there's some writing on this patient's foot.'

Famous surgeon: 'Ah, yes! That's a footnote.'

323. Receptionist: 'The doctor is so funny he'll soon have you in stitches.'

Patient: 'I hope not – I only came in for a check up.'

324. Worried woman: 'Doctor, I think I'm pregnant.'

Doctor: 'But I gave you the Pill.'

Worried woman: 'Yes, I know. But it keeps falling out.'

325. Pretty young nurse: 'Doctor, every time I take this young man's pulse it gets much faster. Should I give him a sedative or something?'

Doctor: 'No. Just give him a blindfold.'

DOGS

326. It was one of the strangest-looking dogs they had ever seen at the pub, and the regulars found it a great topic of conversation.

Eventually, one of them sidled over to the dog's owner and said: 'That's an odd-looking dog you've got there. Is it some sort of guard dog?'

'Yes,' replied the owner.

'Well,' said the man, 'it may be big but I bet you my

Alsatian is more fearsome as its bark is much louder than any noise your dog could make.'

'OK,' agreed the owner of the odd-looking dog. 'I bet you twenty pounds that my dog can make a louder, more scary noise than your dog.'

The man accepted the bet and the Alsatian was encouraged to bark. But the strange-looking dog let out a tremendous roar that shook the whole pub and would certainly have frightened even the bravest criminal.

As the Alsatian's owner admitted defeat he said: 'Your dog can certainly make a noise. But I still think it's odd-looking.'

'Yes,' agreed the owner, 'and it looked even odder until I shaved its mane off.'

327. Two dogs were walking along the pavement. Suddenly, one dog stopped and said: 'My name is Bonzo. What's your name?'

The other dog scratched and thought for a bit, and then replied: 'Well, I think it's Get Down Boy.'

328. When my friend's dog was faced with four trees he didn't have a leg to stand on.

329. Henrietta: 'Whenever we go out we let our puppy stay at home to look after the children.'

Clara: 'Is that safe?'

Henrietta: 'Of course. It's a baby setter.'

330. Man: 'I took my dog to the vet today because it bit my wife.'

Friend: 'Did you have it put to sleep?'

Man: 'No, of course not – I had its teeth sharpened.'

331. 'My dog plays chess with me.'

'That's amazing! It must be a really intelligent animal.'

'Not really. I've won three games to two so far this evening.'

332. 'I've just lost my dog.'
'Why don't you put an advertisement in the paper?'
'Don't be silly – my dog can't read.'

333. Man: 'My dog has got no tail.'
Friend: 'How do you know when it's happy?'
Man: 'When it stops biting me.'

334. 'That's a lovely bulldog you've got there.'
'No, it's not a bulldog – it was chasing a cat and ran into a wall.'

335. 'My dog has got no nose.'
'How does it smell?'
'Terrible.'

336. 'I think John's new dog is a pedigree.'
'What makes you think that?'
'Because it barks in a posh accent.'

337. Man: 'Where's your dog?'
Friend: 'I've had it put down.'
Man: 'Was it mad?'
Friend: 'Well, it wasn't exactly pleased.'

DOLPHINS
338. Dolphins are so intelligent that within only a few weeks of being in captivity they can train a man to stand on the very edge of their pool and throw them fish three times a day.

DREAMS
339. Simon was becoming worried about his ever-increasing weight. One day in his club he happened to mention this to his friend, Peter.
'I can recommend a very good doctor,' said Peter. 'I owe

my slimness all to Dr Frank Einstein. He's invented these marvellous pills which I take.'

'It sounds quite amazing,' said Simon. 'But how do they work?'

'It's really psychological. Every night I take two of the pills just before going to sleep and I always dream about being on a South Sea island, surrounded by hordes of beautiful young native girls. And every day I chase them all around the island and when I wake up I seem to have sweated off a few ounces of surplus fat. It's incredible – and enjoyable!'

The following day Simon went to see Dr Einstein and begged him to give him the same tablets as he was giving Peter. The doctor agreed, and within a few weeks Simon was much thinner.

'How are you finding the treatment?' asked Dr Einstein, when Simon called in for his regular check-up.

'It's very good. But I do have one complaint.'

'Oh, and what is that?'

'The pills you gave my friend Peter made him have wonderful dreams about chasing young native girls all over an island. But all I seem to get is the same horrible nightmare – being chased all over the island by hungry cannibals. Why can't I have pleasant dreams like Peter?'

'Because,' replied the doctor, 'Peter is a private patient – and you are National Health.'

DRIVING INSTRUCTOR
340. Driving instructor: 'What would you do if you were coming down that very steep hill into town and your brakes failed?'

Lady learner: 'Hit something cheap?'

DRUNKS
341. The landlord of a pub frequented by an extremely heavy drinker opened up one day, and in walked a pink

elephant, a green rhinoceros and several orange striped crocodiles. 'I'm sorry,' said the publican, 'I'm afraid he isn't in yet.'

342. The fire engine careered around the corner, and sped off up the road, bells clanging, just as a drunk was staggering out of a pub. He promptly chased after the fire engine, but soon collapsed, exhausted, after only a few hundred yards.

'All right,' he sobbed. 'You can keep your rotten ice lollies!'

343. A drunk came across a man doing press ups in the park, so he said: 'Excuse me, I think someone has stolen your girlfriend.'

344. The drunk came tottering out of a pub and found a man selling tortoises.

'How much are they?' asked the drunk.

'Only ten pounds each,' replied the man.

'I'll take one,' said the drunk, and after he had paid for the tortoise he took it and staggered off.

After twenty minutes, the drunk came swaying up to the tortoise seller and bought another tortoise before teetering away again.

Fifteen minutes later the drunk returned to the tortoise seller. 'You know,' he said, as he bought yet another tortoise, 'they're very expensive – but, by jove, I really love your crunchy pies!'

345. The drunk staggered along the street with a large bottle of brandy in each pocket when he suddenly tripped and fell heavily to the ground.

As he began to pull himself to his feet he noticed that part of him felt wet. He touched the wet patch with his fingers, then looked blearily at his fingers and sighed: 'Thanksh goodnesh! It'sh only blood.'

E

ELECTRICIAN

346. Mrs Smith: 'Why have you come today? You were supposed to repair the doorbell yesterday.'

Electrician: 'I did come yesterday but after I rang three times and got no answer I thought you must be out.'

ELEPHANTS

347. Why has an elephant got Big Ears?

Because Noddy refuses to pay the ransom money.

348. Simon: 'How do you make an elephant fly?'

Clara: 'Use a very large zip.'

349. 'What's the difference between a postbox and an elephant?'

'I don't know.'

'Well, I'm not giving you any letters to post.'

ELF

350. One of the elves was getting rather fat so his wife sent him away to the Elf Farm.

ENEMIES

351. It was in the days of old when the man came riding into the noble's castle at great speed. As soon as his horse had entered the inner courtyard of the castle, the man leapt off his horse and ran to the noble's reception room.

'Sire! Sire! I and my men have done as you wished and pillaged and terrorised in the North.'

'Fool!' snapped the noble. 'I told you to pillage and terrorise in the West. I have no enemies in the North.'

'Sire!' replied the man, 'You do now.'

ENTHUSIASM

352. Mark: 'I throw myself into everything I do.'
Sally: 'Go and dig a large hole.'

ESKIMOS

353. What do you call an Eskimo wearing five balaclavas?
Anything you like, because he can't hear you.

354. The Eskimo set off in his kayak when he met his Cockney Eskimo friend. The Eskimo said he was very cold and so he made a fire in the bottom of his kayak, but the kayak soon burst into flames and the Eskimo had to be rescued by his friend.

'Why did my kayak go up in flames like that?' asked the Eskimo.

'Simple!' replied his friend. 'You can't hope to have your kayak and 'eat it.'

ESTATE AGENT

355. Estate agent to young house-hunting couple: 'First you tell me what you can afford. Then we'll have a good laugh about it and go on from there.'

EXCUSES

356. Charles was on his way home from the office when his car broke down in a small, winding lane. As he began to walk towards the farmhouse in the distance where he hoped to be able to telephone for help, a bright yellow sports car screeched to a halt.

'Can I help?' asked a gorgeous young lady in the sports car.

Charles explained the situation and the young lady explained that she lived in a small village about five miles away. She would take him home, offer him dinner, and he could phone a garage from her house.

Charles readily accepted her offer – including the dinner invitation – and thus it was that he eventually got his car repaired and arrived back home in the early hours of the morning.

'Where do you think you've been?' screamed his wife. 'Out all hours, no thought about me . . .'

'The car broke down and I was helped out by a gorgeous young girl in a sports car and I ended up having dinner with her at her house and then . . .'

'Don't say any more!' shrieked his wife. 'I've had enough of your lies. You've been out with the lads again playing cards!'

EXECUTIVES
357. The managing director's son had just died and as the managing director was without any other heirs there was a mad scramble amongst the executives of the company to take the son's place – even though the son had not yet been laid to rest.

One of the executives was so ambitious that he called on the managing director to express his sympathy at the sad loss of such a great man. But he continued: 'No one could ever hope to achieve as much as your son has done – but I wondered, sir, if it would be possible for me to take his place.'

'Certainly,' replied the managing director. 'I'll see if the undertaker can arrange it.'

358. The television company decided to make a programme about successful business executives, so they called five of them into the studio to talk about their lives and how they managed to be so successful.

The first four executives all told of how they had fought to get to the top – all four of them marrying their respective boss's daughter. But the fifth executive had had a really hard fight to become successful. 'Life was never very easy for me,' he explained. 'I had to fight for everything and times were often extremely difficult – but I just gritted my teeth, rolled up my sleeves . . . and got down to asking Dad to lend me another £500,000.'

F

FARMERS

359. There were two parallel lines of cabbages, so the farmer called it a dual cabbage way.

360. Farmer Brown made his chickens drink lots of whisky. He was hoping that they would lay Scotch eggs.

361. Farmer Smith has just invented a new device which enables him to count his cows in the field quickly. He calls his invention a cowculator.

362. 'This is outrageous!' shouted the middle-aged man to the farmer's wife. 'You charge us a small fortune for camping in your field with absolutely no facilities at all and then one of the bees from one of your hives goes and stings me.'

'Well,' replied the farmer's wife. 'If you can show me which bee it was that stung you, I'll hit it with my husband's cricket bat.'

FEATHERS

363. Young girl: 'If you kiss me it will be a feather in my cap.'

Handsome young man: 'Come outside and I'll make you a Red Indian Chief.'

FILMS

364. I know a man who keeps making films about ducks. He seems to be hooked on making duckumentaries.

FLEAS

365. The male flea said to the pretty female flea: 'Come up and see my itchings.'

366. The two fleas were just leaving the theatre when the male flea turned to the female flea and said: 'Shall we walk, or take a dog?'

367. The old flea was travelling to the cinema on his snail when he was overtaken by a young flea tearing along on a slug.

'What has happened to your old snail?' asked the old flea.

'Oh,' shouted the young flea, gradually disappearing into the distance, 'I thought I'd part exchange it for a convertible.'

FLOWERS

368. 'Darling, I'm afraid the florist made a mistake over my anniversary order for you and they've given me these large Brazilian ferns instead of your favourite anemones.'

'That's all right, dear. They're beautiful! With fronds like these who needs anemones?'

FOOD AND DRINK

369. 'Darling, can I have some undercooked chips, some goocy, cold beans and a fried egg coated in old grease?'

'Of course not, dearest, I couldn't possibly give you anything like that.'

'Why not? That's what you gave me yesterday.'

370. Nightclub customer: 'Can you give me something long, cold and half full of vodka?'

Barman: 'How about my wife?'

371. 'And how did you find the meat?'

'Oh, I just lifted up a chip and there it was.'

372. 'And how do you like the meat balls?'
'I don't know – I've never been to any.'

373. Candles make light meals.

374. 'Darling,' said Mrs Bloggis to her husband. 'I do hope you'll like the sole. It looked a bit off so I fried it, but that didn't seem to do much to it. So I tried grilling it but it still looked funny. So now I've boiled it.'

375. My aunt believes that the best way to make a Mexican chilli is to take him to Alaska.

376. Sally: 'Mummy, do you like baked apples?'
Mother: 'Yes, of course. Don't you remember, we had them last week. Why do you ask?'
Sally: 'Because the orchard is on fire.'

377. Wife: 'I've made you three different sorts of cake today. Would you like to take your pick?'
Husband: 'No thanks, I'll use the hammer and chisel like always.'

378. Mr Bloggs: 'Darling, I don't know what you put in this soup, but it tastes like dishwater.'
Mrs Bloggs: 'How do you know?'

379. Mother: 'The milk has boiled all over the stove. Just look at the mess! I thought I told you to watch when it boiled over.'
Ten-year-old son: 'I did, mum. It was 12.32.'

380. My husband can only tell jokes after he's drunk a whole bottle of whisky. It seems he has a rye sense of humour.

381. The favourite dessert of barristers and solicitors is sue-it pudding.

382. When I worked in a restaurant in San Francisco in the 1980s I was asked to devise the most original dessert possible. So, being a staunch Republican, I made a mould in the shape of Ronald Reagan and was just about to pour the liquid jelly into it when I was suddenly surrounded by FBI agents. They said they didn't want me to set a President . . .

383. He had jelly in one ear and custard in the other, so he told everyone to speak up as he was a trifle deaf.

384. I eat small pieces of metal every day. It's my staple diet.

385. Henry: 'My wife made me a very unusual dinner last night: toad-in-the-hole.'
  Claude: 'What's so unusual about that?'
  Henry: 'She used real toads.'
  Claude: 'Thank goodness she didn't try to make spotted dick . . .'

386. The owners of the small zoo were not doing very well and as they eventually used up all their savings they were forced to start eating some of the animals from their collection.
  One day, when the husband came home carrying two baby monkeys and one small dead bird his wife said: 'Oh no! Surely you don't expect me to cook finch and chimps again!'

FOOTBALL
387. A man and his wife went to the ticket office at Plymouth football ground and handed over a twenty pound note, and said: 'Two, please.'
  'Thank you,' replied the man in the ticket office. 'Would you like the goalkeeper and the centre forward – or are there two other players you'd like to buy instead?'

388. Football player: 'I don't know what to say. I feel so ashamed for missing that goal, I could kick myself.'

Football Club Manager: 'Let me do it for you – you're sure to miss.'

389. My wife refuses to watch football matches as she says they're too political – there's always someone playing at left wing.

G

GAMBLING

390. The compulsive gambler at the roulette table was having a particularly bad run of luck when suddenly he heard a soft, ghostly voice in his ear say 'Number Seven'.

The gambler furtively looked behind him, but there was no one near him who could possibly have made such a ghostly whisper. The gambler decided he had nothing to lose by backing the advice of the mysterious whisperer.

The number came up – number seven had won the gambler a small sum of money – but not enough to cover his earlier losses, so the gambler continued at the table. Again, the ghostly voice whispered 'Number Seven', and the gambler followed the advice and won yet again.

This went on for some considerable time. Just before the gambler placed each bet the ghostly voice would whisper: 'Number Seven', and the number seven always came up.

After this had happened nine times in succession, the gambler had collected quite a number of interested spectators – as well as winning well over five thousand pounds.

Then the ghostly voice whispered: 'Put everything on Number Five'. The gambler was surprised at the change in directions, but he decided to continue to follow the advice given him by the strange, ghostly voice.

The roulette wheel spun round, the gambler held his breath, the crowd around the table watched with astonishment – and the ball landed in number seven. And the ghostly voice in the gambler's ear said 'Damn!'

GARDENING

391. My daughter has a foolproof method of telling whether or not a plant is a weed. She pulls up everything in the garden and then she knows that whatever comes up again must be a weed.

392. Amanda: 'Why are you putting that evil-smelling green powder all over your garden?'
Annabel: 'To keep the crocodiles off it.'
Amanda: 'But there aren't any crocodiles around here!'
Annabel: 'See how good the green powder is?'

393. He's such a lazy gardener the only thing he grows in his garden is old.

394. Two little boys were looking out of the window when they saw a lorry drive past loaded with turf.
'That's what I shall do when I'm rich,' said one of the little boys. 'I'll send my grass away to be cut, too.'

GERMS

395. 'Did you know that deep breathing kills germs?'
'Yes. But how do you get them to breathe deeply?'

GIRLFRIENDS

396. Henry used to go out with a girl who was very class conscious. He didn't have any class and she was very conscious of it.

397. I once had a girlfriend who was so ugly the only people who ever asked her to go to bed were her parents.

398. John's latest girlfriend is called 'Doorknob' – because she's been handled by so many men.

399. Claude's new girlfriend thinks that oral contraception is when she talks her way out of it.

400. My girlfriend knows if she's been sleepwalking: she wakes up in her own bed.

GOLDFISH

401. The philosophical goldfish swam around in his bowl, then stopped for a few seconds and turned to his companion and asked: 'Do you believe in the existence of God?'

'Yes,' replied the second goldfish. 'Who else do you suppose changes our water?'

402. Little Sarah's Aunt Hetty had arrived for tea and Hetty was rather concerned at Sarah's staring.

'Why do you keep staring at me, and then glaring at the goldfish bowl?' asked Aunt Hetty.

'Well I'm watching you and the goldfish bowl because I don't want to miss it when you do what I heard mummy and daddy whispering about: when you drink like a fish.'

GOLF

403. My wife claims that her golf game is improving because today she hit the ball in one.

404. Andrew came rushing into the clubhouse in a state of great agitation. 'I've just sliced the ball into a tree but it re-bounded and went into the road where it hit the rider of a motorbike who fell off his bike and then a lorry ran into him causing its load of onions to spill all over the road which has caused more cars to crash and there are bodies and smashed vehicles all over the place. What can I do?'

The Club President thought deeply for a moment and

then suggested: 'Take it a bit easier on the backswing in future.'

405. After his last shot, Mr Smith turned to his caddy and asked: 'What do you think of my game?'

The caddy thought for a moment and then replied: 'I think your game is quite good. But I still prefer golf myself.'

406. Howard and Horace were playing golf when, by the side of the tenth hole, Horace suddenly stopped playing and watched a hearse and funeral procession drive slowly along a nearby road. As he watched, he lowered his head and took off his cap.

'That was very noble of you,' said Howard.

'Not at all,' replied Horace. 'A husband should always show some respect when his wife dies.'

GRANDMOTHERS

407. 'Granny, can you do an impersonation of a frog?' asked three-year-old Sarah.

'Why?' asked Granny.

'Because,' replied Sarah. 'I heard mummy and daddy talking and they said we'd get a small fortune when you croak.'

408. Millicent was growing very rapidly and her mother was very proud of this and so wrote and told Millicent's grandmother that Millicent had grown another foot since the last time she had seen her.

Almost by return of post, Millicent's grandmother sent her another sock.

GRAVE DIGGER

409. The eminent surgeon was walking through his local churchyard one day when he saw the grave digger having a rest and drinking from a bottle of beer.

'Hey, you!' called the surgeon. 'How dare you laze about and drink alcohol in the churchyard! Get on with your job, or I shall complain to the vicar.'

'I should have thought you'd be the last person to complain,' said the grave digger, 'bearing in mind all your blunders I've had to cover up.'

H

HAIR

410. John: 'When I proposed to you and we got married your hair was blonde. Now it's dark brown.'

Sally: 'So? Dark brown is my natural hair colour.'

John: 'I know that, now. I was just wondering if I could sue you for bleach of promise . . .'

HAMSTERS

411. The man was lonely so he went to his local pet shop and asked for an animal that would make a good companion for him as he was allergic to birds and fish. The pet shop owner recommended a hamster, so the man bought two hamsters, some hamster food, and a special cage.

The next day the man was back in the pet shop. 'Those two hamsters you sold me have died. There must have been something wrong with them. Can I have two more, please?'

The pet shop owner gave him two more hamsters and the man left the shop. But next day the man returned and said: 'This is ridiculous! The two hamsters you gave me yesterday fell down and died this morning. I'll buy your entire stock of hamsters – then perhaps I might get two that will live a reasonable length of time – and perhaps even breed and keep me amused.'

The pet shop owner sold the man his complete stock of hamsters – all fifty-eight of them – and the man left the pet shop.

Two days later the pet shop owner was horrified to find the man in his shop again. 'All the hamsters have died,' said the man. 'I don't want anything to do with animals ever again – they just seem to curl up and die just to spite me. But it seems a pity to waste all the hamster bodies – is there anything you can suggest to do with them? It seems horrible to have to throw them in the dustbin.'

'Well,' said the pet shop owner, 'if you mash them all up and then boil them until you get a sort of gooey stuff, this makes excellent fertiliser for the garden.'

The man left the shop and went home to follow the pet shop owner's instructions. But a week later the man was back in the pet shop. 'I really must congratulate you on your excellent suggestion,' said the man. 'I did as you suggested with the hamster bodies and in no time at all I had seven gigantic beanstalks in my garden. In fact, they were so high I had to stick red lights on top of them to warn aeroplanes to keep away. That hamster mixture really is amazing stuff for beanstalks.'

'You know,' said the pet shop owner. 'That's incredible. You usually get Tulips From Hamster Jam.'

HANDWRITING
412. Claude's teacher said his handwriting was so bad the only profession he could follow on leaving school was to be a doctor.

HEARING AID
413. Cuthbert: 'I've just bought this amazing miracle of modern science – a hearing aid as small as a pea.'

Rodney: 'Was it very expensive?'

Cuthbert: 'It's almost one o'clock.'

HEDGEHOG
414. Hedgehog finding itself on top of a scrubbing brush: 'We all make mistakes, don't we?'

HEREAFTER

415. The small car pulled up to a sudden halt. 'Have you run out of petrol?' asked the girl, somewhat sarcastically.

'No, of course not,' replied her young boyfriend.

'Then why have we stopped?'

'You will no doubt have noticed that we are parked in a secluded spot in the middle of this forest and miles from anywhere – so I thought you might like a discussion about the hereafter.'

'That's something new,' replied the young girl. 'What do you mean?'

'Simple! If you're not hereafter, what I'm hereafter, you'll be hereafter I've gone.'

HISTORICAL

416. 'Apart from *that*, Mrs Lincoln, how did you enjoy the play?'

417. At the time of the French Revolution many people went completely off their heads.

418. During the late nineteenth century some South American rebels had been rounded up by government forces.

On the day set for their execution it was pouring with rain as the soldiers marched the rebels to the field where they were to be shot.

'It's not right that we should die,' complained one of the rebels.

'Shut up!' snapped a soldier. 'Think yourself lucky you don't have to walk back to prison in this weather.'

419. 'Now, how much would *you* like to contribute to the Indian Relief Fund, Mrs Custer?'

420. With the Gaul having been captured, Caesar decided to put him in the Arena to fight.

First he was matched against a hungry lion, but the Gaul calmly picked up the animal as it rushed towards him, whirled it around in the air by its tail, and then smashed its head in.

The promoters of the fight were annoyed, so the Gaul was given a choice: either fight a pack of lions or enter into combat with their best gladiator.

But the promoters knew the audience wanted to see blood – the blood of the Gaul – so as a slight handicap the man was buried up to his neck in sand. The gladiator approached, drew his six foot long sword, raised it above the Gaul's head – to an enormous cheer from the audience – then brought it down, but the Gaul moved his head to one side so the sword hit the ground.

The crowd rose to their feet, jeering and shouting: 'Fight fair, you coward!'

421. Then there was the ancient fireplace salesman – Alfred the *Grate*!'

422. Paul Revere came thundering up to a small farmhouse during his historic ride from Boston to Lexington. The young farmer's wife came to the door.

'Get ya husband,' yelled Revere, 'We gotta fight the English.'

'My husband ain't home,' she replied, trembling.

'Get ya sons and kinfolk,' he yelled.

'I ain't got no sons nor kinfolk.'

'Ain't nobody at home?'

'Nope!'

'Whoah, boy! Can I interest you in buying some insurance?'

HOLIDAYS
423. 'Mummy, Mummy! Where are you?' cried the little boy on the promenade at Bournemouth.

'You poor little boy,' said an elderly lady. 'Come with me

and I'll get you an ice cream and then we'll go and look for your mummy and if we still can't find her I'll take you to the nice man who rents out the beach huts and he'll get the police to look for your mummy.'

'I know where your mummy is,' said a small girl. 'She's . . .'

'Shush!' whispered the little boy. 'I know where she is, too, but this way I've already had two free ice creams this morning from other people before we found my mother – don't be mean and stop me getting a third one!'

424. The world-famous lawyer was holidaying on an expensive yacht when he fell overboard into a group of sharks. They declined to eat him out of professional courtesy.

425. Two middle-aged men were sitting at a beach-side café sipping lager when one of the men said: 'Hey! Look at that fat frump in the green costume. The one jumping up and down in the sea and waving. Most hideous sight on the entire beach. Do you think all that jumping up and down and beckoning and leering towards me is some kind of propositioning?'

'I don't know,' said the other man, 'If you like, I'll go down there and ask her: she's my wife!'

426. The weather was terrible for the whole two weeks of my holiday. I didn't get brown from the sun, but from the rust caused by the rain.

427. A holiday is something you have for two weeks that takes fifty weeks to pay for.

428. Jacintha: 'How was your holiday in Switzerland? Did you like the scenery?'

Sarah: 'Not really. You couldn't see much as the mountains kept getting in the way.'

429. Four-year-old Lionel: 'Mummy, can you buy me a metal detector, please?'

Mother: 'Why do you want one?'

Lionel: 'I'm hoping to find Daddy's watch with it.'

Mother: 'I didn't know Daddy had lost his watch.'

Lionel: 'He hasn't. But I was hoping if I had a metal detector and it picked up where Daddy's watch was buried that would also show me where I've buried Daddy in the sand.'

430. Two little boys were paddling in the sea at Margate.

'Coo, ain't your feet dirty,' said one little boy.

'Yes,' replied the other, 'we didn't come last year.'

431. An Irishman working in an Arab country where alcohol was banned was stopped at the Customs counter after returning from a holiday in France.

'What's this in this bottle?' asked the customs officer, taking out a large bottle from the Irishman's suitcase.

'Oh,' said the Irishman, 'that is only Holy Water from Lourdes.'

'Hmmm!' muttered the customs officer as he took the top off the bottle and sniffed the liquid inside. Then he tasted some of it. 'It looks, smells and tastes very much like whisky to me, sir.'

'Glory be!' replied the Irishman, ''tis another miracle!'

432. Bernard was on holiday abroad and decided to visit the local bazaar.

'Want to buy the genuine skull of Moses?' asked a stall owner.

'Not really,' replied Bernard. 'It's much too expensive.'

'What about this skull,' said the stall-owner, producing another skull. 'This is much cheaper, because it's smaller – the skull of Moses as a child.'

433. Local: 'Lady! I'd come out of that sea if I were you. There are lots of sharks about.'

Lady tourist: 'That's all right. They're only man-eating sharks.'

434. Simon: 'I know of only one way that a girl can remain a good girl on holiday in Greece.'
Hazel: 'And what way is that?'
Simon: 'I was right! I thought you wouldn't know.'

435. The last time I went on holiday for a fortnight it only rained twice: the first time for seven days, and the second time for a week.

436. For the first time in twenty years, Mr and Mrs Jones decided to take their holidays apart from each other. Mrs Jones went to visit relatives in the USA while Mr Jones went to Thailand.

The weather in Thailand was fantastic and Mr Jones had a wonderful time, especially after he met a sexy young Thai massage girl called Sunny.

Indeed, the girl and the location must have gone to his head as he sent a postcard to his wife on which he wrote: 'The weather is here. Wish you were Sunny.'

HOLLYWOOD
437. Two little boys were talking in Hollywood. 'What's your new dad like?' asked one.

'Oh, he's OK, I guess,' replied the other. 'Have you met him?'

'Yeah!' said the first boy. 'We had him last year.'

HOMESICK
438. Janice: 'I'm feeling rather homesick.'
George: 'But you *are* at home!'
Janice: 'I know. But I'm sick of it.'

HORSES

439. My horse likes to gamble. Every time we come to a fence or a gate he tosses me for it.

440. Claire: 'Mummy, is it true that horses have six legs?'

Mother: 'Whatever makes you think that?'

Claire: 'Well, I heard that a horse has forelegs at the front and two at the back.'

HOSPITAL

441. Nurse: 'Well, Mr Mitchell, you seem to be coughing much more easily this morning.'

Mr Mitchell, groaning in his bed: 'That's because I've been practising all night.'

442. Visitor: 'Excuse me, but can you tell me which ward Vera Ogglebuggy is in.'

Receptionist: 'Ah, yes. Wasn't she the lady who was run down by a steamroller earlier this morning?'

Visitor: 'Yes.'

Receptionist: 'Well, she's in Wards 7, 8, 9, 10 and 11.'

443. Voice on the phone: 'Hello? Is that the maternity hospital?'

Receptionist: 'Yes.'

Voice on the phone: 'Can you please send an ambulance round, the wife is about to have a baby.'

Receptionist: 'Is this her first baby?'

Voice on the phone: 'No. This is her husband.'

HOTELS

444. It was one o'clock in the morning and the manager of the hotel had just been woken up by a frantic phone call from a little old lady. 'Come quickly! Oh, please come quickly!' she wailed. 'I can see a naked man from my window.'

The manager hastily dressed and rushed up to the little old lady's room. He found her pointing at a block of flats opposite her hotel bedroom – but all the manager could see was the naked top half of a young man.

'But my dear woman,' soothed the manager, 'the young man opposite is surely only preparing for bed. And how can you possibly be offended by him? The man may not be completely naked.'

'The wardrobe!' shrieked the little old lady. 'Stand on the wardrobe.'

445. Notice in a foreign hotel: 'The water in this establishment is completely hygienic – it has all been passed by the manager.'

446. I once stayed at a hotel in Venice that was so damp there was a goldfish in the mousetrap!

447. The beautiful young girl was lying naked on the roof of her expensive hotel, sunbathing. Suddenly the manager came up to her, coughed slightly, then said: 'Excuse me, madam, but this is hardly the place for nudity.'

'Why not?' asked the girl. 'I can't see anyone.'

'That may be so,' replied the manager, 'but you are lying on the skylight over the dining room and it is now lunch time.'

I

IDENTITY PARADE
448. At one identity parade in Ireland fifteen people were made to stand in a line – and then a pickpocket was brought in and asked to point out which people he'd robbed.

IMPRESSIONS
449. Jim's wife was chatting to her friend about Jim's boss, who at that moment was regaling the party with details of his war experiences in Egypt.

'I believe he's great at doing impressions,' commented the friend.

'Yes,' agreed Jim's wife. 'Right now he's doing his impression of a river – small at the head and big at the mouth.'

450. Three-year-old Clara likes to do bird impressions – she eats worms.

INLAND REVENUE
451. The frantic-looking lady came rushing out of her house into the street and cried: 'Help! Help! My young son has swallowed a coin and is choking. I don't know what to do!'

The people in the street all looked the other way, except for one middle-aged gentleman who rushed into the lady's house, found her young son, turned him upside down and shook him until the coin fell out of his mouth.

'Oh, thank you!' cried the lady, in happiness. 'Are you a doctor?'

'No, madam,' replied the middle-aged man. 'I'm with the Inland Revenue.'

452. The income tax authorities have now produced a new, simple tax form with only two sections: (a) How much do you earn? (b) Send it.

453. The tax inspector received an income tax return from a bachelor executive claiming a dependent son. He thought this was rather odd, so he sent back the form with a note stating: 'This must be a typist's error.'

Back came the form from the executive, together with a pencilled marginal comment next to the inspector's, saying: 'You're telling me!'

INSECTS
454. Little Wilhelmina was in the garden when she asked: 'Dad – what are those two insects doing?'

'Well,' said her father, 'you know what I told you about the birds and bees – that's what they are doing.'

'But they are not birds and bees.'

'I know – they're called daddy-longlegs.'

'Oh!' said Wilhelmina, and paused to think about this for a while. Then she said: 'So one is a mummy-longlegs and the other a daddy-longlegs.'

'No,' replied her father. 'They're both daddy-longlegs.'

Wilhelmina thought for a while, then stamped on the insects.

'What did you do that for?' asked her father, somewhat surprised.

'I'm not having *that* sort of thing in *our* garden,' said Wilhelmina, firmly.

455. A friend of mine has just invented a wonderful new insecticide. You spray it on all your plants and it promptly kills them so that the insects will then starve to death.

INSURANCE

456. I've just bought a retirement policy. If I keep paying the premiums for thirty-five years the insurance salesman can retire rich.

457. When Mr Smith read the small print on his double indemnity policy he discovered that if he died he would be buried twice.

458. Insurance salesman: 'Surely your husband needs more life insurance? I mean, if your husband suddenly dropped dead, what would you do?'
  Mrs Smith: 'I'd probably get a pet dog instead.'

INVESTMENT

459. Brian: 'You must think I'm absolutely stupid, asking me to invest in such a crackpot scheme.'
  Fred: 'So I can put you down for a few thousand, then . . .'

ITCH

460. Mother: 'Why are you scratching yourself?'
  Three-year-old Anna: 'Because only I know where I itch.'

J

JACUZZI

461. The first time a friend of mine went into a jacuzzi he thought he'd had a sudden attack of wind.

JOBS

462. Millicent: 'My husband's career is in ruins.'

Mary: 'Oh, I'm sorry to hear that.'

Millicent: 'There's nothing to be sorry about. He's an archaeologist.'

463. 'Now,' said the interviewer, 'before we start the interview proper I'd like you to take an intelligence test.'

'An intelligence test?' queried the job applicant. 'The advertisement in the newspaper didn't mention intelligence – it stated you were looking for a research assistant for an MP.'

464. John: 'I hear that you've just joined a company selling lifts. How's business?'

Fred: 'Oh, up and down.'

465. When Peter left school he went to the parks department and asked if he could be trained to be a rubbish collector.

'But you don't need training for that,' said the parks superintendent. 'You just pick it up as you go along.'

466. Do manufacturers of rope have all their assets tied up?

467. My wife has recently got a job that takes a lot of guts. She makes guitar strings.

468. Mr and Mrs Smith were interviewing applicants for the job of cook for their country house.

One applicant seemed well suited for the job and he particularly appealed to Mrs Smith because he was young and attractive.

'Tell me,' said Mr Smith. 'What if my wife asked for a little extra after dinner? Would you be able to cope?'

The applicant smiled and said: 'Of course. I'm just as liberated as you two seem to be: I've had a vasectomy.'

JOURNALISTS
469. He's such a terrible journalist. The only time he gets scoops is when he's being served ice-cream.

470. 'Robert!' shouted the editor of the local newspaper. 'Did you get that story about the man who sings bass and soprano at the same time?'

'There's no story, sir,' replied Robert, the young reporter. 'The man has two heads.'

JUMBLE SALE
471. I once went to a jumble sale and bought a very old and very large bureau. While I was cleaning it I must have pressed a secret button and a large panel in the back of the bureau popped open and three people fell out shouting: 'Where am I? Where am I?' That's how I realised I must have bought a missing persons bureau.

K

KANGAROO

472. One enterprising Australian farmer tried to cross a kangaroo with a sheep so he would get a woolly jumper.

473. The mother kangaroo suddenly leapt into the air and gave a cry of pain and anguish. 'Sidney!' she screamed. 'How many more times do I have to tell you that you cannot smoke in bed!'

KIDNAPPING

474. Did you hear about the doctor who tried to be a kidnapper? He failed because no one could read his ransom letters.

475. Sally: 'Did you hear about the kidnapping this afternoon?'

Simon: 'No – who was it?'

Sally: 'My kid sister. She was napping and mum woke her up!'

KNOCK KNOCK

476. 'Knock, knock.'

'Who's there?'

'Irish stew.'

'Irish stew who?'

'Irish stew in the name of the law.'

477. 'Knock, knock.'
'Who's there?'
'You're a lady.'
'You're a lady who?'
'I didn't know you could yodel.'

L

LANDLORD

478. The young man walked into the pet shop and asked if he could buy 387 beetles, 18 rats and five mice.

'I'm sorry, sir, but we can only supply the mice. But what did you want all the other creatures for?' asked the pet shop manager.

'I was thrown out of my flat this morning,' replied the young man. 'And my landlord says I must leave the place exactly as I found it.'

LAS VEGAS

479. The easiest way to return from Las Vegas with a small fortune is to go there with a very large fortune.

LAUGHTER

480. What goes 'ha ha, hee hee, bonk'?
Someone laughing his head off.

LEGAL

481. The judge was only four feet three inches tall – a small thing sent to try us.

LIARS

482. Man: 'That damn wife of mine is a liar!'
Friend: 'How do you know?'

Man: 'Because she said she spent the night with Claire.'
Friend: 'So?'
Man: '*I* spent the night with Claire.'

483. Women are to blame for all the lying men do – they will insist on continually asking questions.

LIFE GUARD
484. Beach inspector: 'Why have you applied for the job of beach guard? You're just wasting my time! You can't even swim!'

Job applicant: 'I know. But at seven feet two inches in height I can wade out quite a long way!'

LION
485. One day the lion woke up feeling better than he had ever done before. He felt so fit and healthy he could beat the world. So he rose proudly and went for a prowl in the jungle. Soon he came across a snake and the lion stopped.

'Who is the king of the jungle?' asked the lion.

'You, of course,' replied the snake, and slithered away.

Next, the lion came to a small pool where he found a crocodile.

'Who is the king of the jungle?'

'Why, you are,' replied the crocodile and slid into the murky depths of the water.

This went on all morning, all the animals agreeing that the lion was the king of the jungle. Then he came across an elephant.

'Who is the king of the jungle?' asked the lion.

In reply, the elephant picked up the lion with its trunk, hurled the lion around in the air and then dropped him on the ground.

'All right, all right,' groaned the battered lion. 'There's no need to get angry just because you don't know the answer.'

LUMBERJACK

486. James was a very old man and when he turned up at a Canadian lumberjacks' camp and asked if he could help in chopping down the trees no one would take him seriously.

'Let me show you how good I am,' begged the old man.

Eventually, the lumberjack boss got tired of the old man's whining and pleading and gave James an axe, saying: 'Don't try too hard, old man. We don't want you killing yourself.'

James took the axe and went over to one of the tallest trees near the camp. The lumberjacks were amazed to see the old man chop away at the tree with enormous speed, and within only a few minutes the tree was lying on the ground.

'That's amazing!' said the lumberjack boss. 'Where did you learn to chop trees down like that?'

'I got my basic training in the Sahara,' replied the old man.

'But there aren't any trees in the Sahara,' said the lumberjack boss.

'That's right,' replied the old man. 'But there used to be until I started training.'

M

MAGICIAN

487. A magician on board a cruise ship used to do amazing tricks every night in the cabaret spot – but the captain's pet parrot always used to shout 'Phoney, phoney!' at the end of the magician's act.

Then one day the ship hit an iceberg and sank, but the magician and the parrot managed to cling to a piece of wood and float clear of the sinking ship.

After a few days of floating, the parrot turned an inquisitive beak to the magician and said: 'OK, genius. What have you done with the ship?'

MAIL ORDER

488. Henrietta (talking on the phone): 'Can I speak to someone in the mail order department?'

Voice on phone: 'Speaking.'

Henrietta: 'Oh. I'd like to order one. About thirty to thirty-five, fairly tall, reasonably well-off, and who likes animals.'

MARRIED LIFE

489. Married man: 'In your sermon this morning, vicar, you said it was wrong for people to profit from other people's mistakes. Do you really agree with that?'

Vicar: 'Of course I do.'

Married man: 'In that case, will you consider refunding the twenty pounds I paid you for marrying me to my wife seven years ago?'

490. The lady was having an argument with her maid. Before leaving the room the maid decided to say exactly what she thought.

'You might like to know,' she said, 'that your husband told me only last week that I am a far better housekeeper and cook than you are. He also said I was much better looking!'

The lady remained silent.

'And that's not all,' continued the maid, 'I'm far better than you in bed.'

'I suppose my husband told you that as well!' snapped the lady.

'No,' replied the maid, 'the gardener did.'

491. 'Why are you in such a hurry?'

'I'm on my way to the doctor – I don't like the look of my wife.'

'Oh! Then I'll come with you – I hate the sight of mine, too.'

492. Henrietta: 'Why is your husband asleep on top of the chandelier?'

Wilhelmina: 'Oh – that's because he's a light sleeper.'

493. My wife treats me like a pagan god. Every evening at dinner time she gives me a burnt offering.

494. Sally: 'I think my husband must have a sixth sense.'
Sarah: 'Why?'
Sally: 'Because there's no sign of the other five.'

495. 'I hear that Dracula wants a divorce.'

'Why is that?'

'Because his wife is reluctant to give him his jugular rights.'

496. 'My wife speaks through her nose.'
'Why?'
'She's worn her mouth out.'

497. After our honeymoon I felt like a new man. My wife said she felt like one, too.

498. A beautiful nineteen-year-old girl was once asked why she had married a fat, balding, sixty-three-year-old man who just happened to be very wealthy and own a number of large period houses. 'It's simple,' she said. 'I married him because I love his beautiful manors.'

499. My wife is so frigid whenever she opens her mouth a little light comes on.

500. I wouldn't say my husband was stupid – but when he went to a mindreader they gave him his money back.

501. My husband is so thin whenever he goes to the park the ducks throw *him* bread.

502. My wife is so bandy she hangs her drawers over a boomerang every night.

503. 'Jean, I think your husband dresses nattily.'
'Natalie who?'

504. My wife, besides being rather fat, is incredibly bossy – always telling people what they should do. One day she was on a bus and had just settled down and got comfortable in her seat when she saw that the only standing passengers were three middle-aged women.

My wife turned to the man sitting next to her and said, in a very loud voice: 'If you were a gentleman, you'd get up and let one of those women sit down.'

'If you were a lady,' said the man, 'you'd get up and let all three of them sit down.'

505. Mrs Smith: 'I've just read an interesting article. It said that most accidents that happen, happen in the kitchen.'

Mr Smith: 'I know: you always expect me to eat them.'

506. David was out all night with the glamorous hostess from a notorious Soho night club. When he returned home at five o'clock in the morning he tried to sneak into bed with his wife without waking her. But he was unsuccessful and she turned on the bedside light and watched her husband undress before putting on his pyjamas.

'Where is your underwear?' she demanded, when it was obvious that David had not been wearing any even before he had started to undress.

'My God!' cried David, in anguish. 'I've been robbed!'

507. Wife: 'Darling what would you do if you came home from the office one day and found me in bed with another man?'

Husband: 'Oh, I'd tell him to go away and beat him over the head with his white stick.'

508. I wouldn't say my wife was promiscuous, but she's been picked up so many times she's beginning to grow handles.

509. That middle-aged couple just across the road from us haven't spoken to each other for four years. It's not because they've had a row; but they just can't think of anything to say.

510. Her husband is a fascinating conversationalist – if you happen to be interested in building model railways out of matchsticks.

511. Janet: 'My husband is no good.'

Julia: 'But I thought you told me last week that he was a model husband?'

Janet: 'He is a model husband – but not a working model.'

512. There's nothing so restful as the sleep of the just – except, perhaps, the sleep of the just after.

513. Algernon: 'I'd like to buy the woman I love a little cottage in the country where we can always be together.'
Cuthbert: 'So why don't you?'
Algernon: 'My wife won't let me.'

514. My husband and I have a perfect marriage based on a give-and-take relationship: he gives and I take.

515. Man: 'My wife and I had a short row on Friday night. She wanted to go to the opera and I wanted to go to the theatre – but we soon came to an agreement.'
Friend: 'And what was the opera like?'

516. At least my wife isn't two-faced. She can't be – otherwise she wouldn't wear that one all the time.

517. And she's got a marvellous old mother. She's 79 and hasn't got one grey hair. She's completely bald.

518. Newly married wife: 'Darling, the woman next door has got a coat exactly like mine.'
Husband: 'I suppose that's a hint that you want a new coat?'
Wife: 'Well, it would be quite a lot cheaper than moving to a new house.'

519. I wouldn't say my wife is continually moaning about being ill, but she's just bought a Do-It-Yourself Embalming Kit.

520. My wife frequently goes for a tramp in the woods – fortunately for him, he always manages to get away.

521. Small boy: 'Mummy, is it true that people can have sixteen marriage partners?'
Mother: 'Whatever gave you that idea?'
Small boy: 'Well, I've just watched that TV play and two

people were getting married and the clergyman said they could have sixteen partners: four better, four worse, four richer and four poorer.'

522. My husband sometimes does the housework. I wouldn't say he pushes much dirt under the carpet – but I have to walk uphill to the fireplace.

523. My wife has a slight impediment in her speech. Every now and then she has to stop to take a breath.

524. When Henry told his wife he was feeling half dead she quickly picked him up, threw him over her shoulder and carried him to the local cemetery where she buried him up to his waist.

525. My wife has a good sense of rumour.

526. Fred: 'I call my wife a peach.'
   John: 'That's nice. Is it because she's soft, sweet and juicy?'
   Fred: 'No. It's because she's got a heart of stone.'

MASSEUSE
527. A friend of mine got a job as a masseuse at a very exclusive health club in London because she wanted to rub shoulders with the rich and famous.

MILITARY MATTERS
528. Sally: 'Did you know that my family has a long military history?'
   Samantha: 'No.'
   Sally: 'Yes. One of my ancestors even fell at Waterloo.'
   Samantha: 'Why – did someone push him off the platform?'

529. General: 'Can you tell me what a soldier must be before he can be buried with full military honours?'

Private: 'Dead, sir.'

530. It was quite a number of years ago when the Italian Army used to fight with spears. Just before one of their greatest battles, the Italian commander assembled his men to give them a stirring speech before they went into battle.

'It does not matter,' he said, 'that the odds are overwhelmingly against us. We are Italians and we shall go forward fighting as only Italians can. Now raise up your spears and come with me into battle. I will lead the way to a glorious victory that shall be ours.'

As the commander picked up his spear and marched bravely forward to meet the enemy, his men laid down their spears, sat on the ground, clapped their hands, and shouted: 'Bravo!'

531. Angela: 'My Dad's got hundreds of medals.'

Alicia: 'He must have been very brave in the last War.'

Angela: 'No – he got them in his job: he's a pawnbroker.'

532. Claude: 'When I grow up I want to be in the army.'

Mother: 'Why? You're only four now and I'm sure you'll change your mind as you get older.'

Claude: 'I won't change my mind. I want to be a soldier.'

Mother: 'But what if you get in a war and have to fight and get killed?'

Claude: 'But who would want to kill me?'

Mother: 'The enemy.'

Claude: 'That's all right, then. I'll be in the enemy army.'

MINDS

533. Michael: 'I've just changed my mind.'

Sally: 'That's good! I hope it's better than your old one.'

534. Two mind-readers met in the street and one said to the other: 'Good morning! You're fine. How am I?'

MISER
535. When Edward called on his friend Arnold (who was something of a miser) he found Arnold carefully stripping the wallpaper.
   'Are you re-decorating?' asked Edward.
   'Of course not!' replied Arnold. 'I'm moving.'

MISSIONARY
536. A missionary went to a remote part of the world to teach some natives. On his travels he came to a small village where he decided to make a speech. It went something like this:
   Missionary: 'All men are your enemies and you must love your enemies.'
   The natives raised their spears and shouted 'Hussanga!'
   Missionary: 'If a man should smite you, turn the other cheek.'
   The natives raised their spears again and shouted 'Hussanga!'
   Missionary: 'Fighting is wrong – you must not fight.'
   Once again, the natives raised their spears and shouted 'Hussanga!'
   The missionary decided he had said enough for one day, and as he made his way off the platform he said to the native nearest to him: 'I think my little speech went down quite well, don't you? You all seemed to agree with it.'
   'Hmm,' said the native. 'Mind you don't tread in the hussanga when you get off the platform.'

537. It was the old missionary in Africa who gave the tribe of cannibals their first taste of Christianity.

MODERN ART
538. Ethel: 'This modern art is so difficult to understand.'

Henrietta: 'Why? It's simple: if you can walk around it then it must be a sculpture, and if they've hung it on the wall then it can only be a picture.'

MOTHS

539. Those mothballs I bought last week aren't very good. The house is still full of moths. Every time I throw a mothball at them they fly out of the way and I've only managed to hit one.

540. Jeremy: 'Why do moths fly with their legs apart?'

Justin: 'I don't know. Why do moths fly with their legs apart?'

Jeremy: 'Have you ever seen the size of a moth ball?'

MOUSE

541. What is the largest species of mouse in the world? A hippapotamouse.

542. What do you get if you cross a mouse with an elephant? Giant holes in the skirting board.

543. A baby mouse saw a bat for the first time in its life and ran home, screaming, to its mother saying it had just seen an angel.

MUMMY, MUMMY!

544. 'Mummy, Mummy! The milkman's at the door. Have you got the money – or shall I go out and play?'

545. 'Mummy! I'm stroking a deer with both hands.'

'I know. You're bambi-dextrous!'

MUSIC

546. Some years ago, when there was still a USSR, Jeremy was a violinist with a British orchestra that was due to perform at a concert in Moscow.

Prior to the concert Jeremy strolled around Moscow and then sat in a park where he decided to study some of the music he was to play that night.

No sooner had he opened his sheet music than he was pounced on by KGB men and hauled off to be interrogated.

Jeremy denied doing anything illegal or subversive but the KGB continued their questioning for several days during which time Jeremy was kept in a small room and given only bread and water as sustenance. Then a KGB officer marched into the room and waved the sheet music at Jeremy.

'It is no good you denying that this is a code,' said the KGB officer. 'Handel has already confessed.'

547. My young daughter's singing is rather like a quiz show – Maim That Tune.

548. Fred: 'What key do you sing in?'
  Geoffrey: 'Chubb or Yale.'

549. What note do you get when you drop a grand piano down a coal mine? A flat miner.

N

NAILS

550. Man: 'I cured my son of biting his nails.'
Friend: 'Oh, how?'
Man: 'Knocked all his teeth out.'

551. Customer: 'Ironmonger! Have you got one inch nails?'
Ironmonger: 'Yes, sir.'
Customer: 'Then please scratch my back, it's itching something awful.'

552. The guest was staring at the child with astonishment as the child busily knocked nails into the expensive Scandinavian furniture in his host's dining-room.

The guest turned to his host and asked: 'Don't you find it expensive to let your son play games like that?'

'Not at all,' replied the host, proudly, 'I get the nails wholesale.'

NELSON

553. Nelson was dying on board HMS *Victory*. He looked up, sadly, and said: 'Kiss me, Hardy!'

Hardy looked down and muttered: 'All these years on the same ship and *now* he asks me!'

NEWS

554. The marriage of two lighthouse keepers was said, this evening, to be on the rocks.

555. A Californian scientist has recently invented saw-edged false teeth for eating canned fruit.

556. Eggs are going up – the hens have lost all sense of direction.

557. Missing: three old ladies – believed to be locked in a lavatory.

558. Owing to a strike at the meteorological office, there will be no weather tomorrow.

559. A man swallowed a dud coin late last night. He is expected to be charged with passing counterfeit money later today.

560. In court this morning was a young man accused of peddling drugs. He said he had left his bicycle at home.

561. A man who beat his carpet to death a few hours ago is soon expected to be charged with matricide.

562. The newly elected mayor laid a foundation stone this afternoon. He is not officially recognised as being a chicken.

563. A man tried to stab me early this evening. He was a man after my own heart.

564. A beautiful young typist kissed a prince last night. He turned into a toad.

565. In Moscow early this week, Vladimir Baronovitch lifted over two tons – and earned the title: 'The World's Most Perfectly Ruptured Man.'

566. Speaking about the droppings of pigeons in the town, a council official said: 'We must try not to dodge the issue.'

567. A dumpling was said today to be in a bit of a stew.

568. The plan to wrap all meat pies in tin has been foiled.

569. A man walked through the streets of Southampton today wearing only a newspaper. He said he liked to dress with *The Times*.

570. An inflatable rubber lilo collapsed and died today at its South Harrow home.

571. It has recently been discovered that Wales is sinking into the sea – due to the many leeks in the ground.

572. A strawberry was reported today to be in a bit of a jam.

573. It was reported this afternoon that a man in Cornwall was partially electrocuted. After his recovery the man said: 'It came as something of a shock.'

574. In his bid to become an MP, Mr John Berkeley-Wilson-Hepplewhite has applied for re-election to the human race.

575. On Saturday a fair will be held at the small village of Rotting Green. Most of the visitors will be undertakers so the organisers confidently hope it will be a fête worse than death.

576. A hymn has recently been dedicated to a Birmingham corset factory. It is 'All Is Safely Gathered In.'

577. Police are investigating the theft of 38 dogs from a local kennel. They say they are following a number of leads.

578. Yesterday evening saw the opening of a new play starring that famous actress noted for her snake-like movements, Anna Conder. Her remarkable performance moved many people – to go and visit the bar.

579. A compass has recently complained of going round in circles.

580. Last night an amazing hush fell on the audience at the opening of the new play: 'Nurse Anna Stetic – the thing with the lamp.' It was little William Hush, who had fallen from the balcony.

581. It was the coldest day in Britain yesterday for the past twenty years. At Brighton three mechanics were sitting in a garage, shivering, when they heard a knock at the door. On opening the door, the wind howled past them and they saw a shaking, shivering monkey who looked up and said: 'Excuse me, do you do welding?'

582. A lady dropped her handbag over the edge of a railway platform this morning. The porters refused to retrieve the handbag as they considered it beneath their station.

583. Yesterday, five hundred men walked out of a steel mill while it was still in operation. A Union spokesman said they had to strike while the iron was hot.

584. An MP took his seat in the House of Commons today – but he was forced to put it back.

585. A few hours ago two chairmen of rival oil-stove manufacturing companies were involved in a heated argument.

586. The Chairman of a major blotting paper company announced a few minutes ago that he found his work very absorbing.

587. The President of the Periscope Manufacturers' Association said today that business was 'looking up'.

588. On Tuesday a brewery worker fell into a tank of beer and came to a bitter end.

589. The disappearance of some yeast from a Glasgow bakery in the early hours of this morning has given rise to some anxiety.

590. A well-known iron gate manufacturer was said today to be somewhat overwrought.

591. A man was trapped on the roof of a blazing block of flats this evening. He escaped by taking all his clothes off, looking at the astonished audience below, and walking down the stares.

592. A carpet said to a floor today: 'OK. Don't move, I've got you covered.'

593. Not to mention the all-metal noticeboard which commented this morning: 'You can't pin anything on me.'

594. A Scotsman was fined for indecent conduct at Edinburgh on Friday. According to witnesses the man had continually wiped the perspiration off his forehead with his kilt.

595. In a speech last night the Prime Minister, in replying to questions, said it was not true that old people were living from hand to mouth – it was just that they had to do without the luxuries of life – such as television, housing, clothing, food . . .'

596. Late last night a large hole was made in the walls surrounding Sunnyview Nudist Camp at Bigglehampton. Police are looking into it.

597. A man jumped into a 482 mile long river in France in the early hours of this morning. He was said to be in Seine.

598. I have just shot some very strange animals that were chewing my typewriter. That is the end of the gnus.

NEWS ANNOUNCEMENTS: 2097

599. Little Puddlington's Arts Festival this year is to include a revolutionary new play in which all the characters remain clothed throughout the entire evening. The audience, however, is expected to strip instead.

600. It was officially announced today that, due to the ever-increasing use of Hyde Park by dogs, the area is now to be designated as a huge open cess pit and play area for dogs. Humans will now be banned from the Park, announced the new mayor, Mr Woof – who, incidentally, is believed to be a small basset hound and only this country's second canine mayor since dogs were given the vote. The first non-human mayor was, of course, the well known Miss Growl of Hove who has represented the town for several years.

601. Mrs Blackhorse has sent a petition of three names to the Prime Minister complaining about the recent comedy programme which included scenes of men wearing trousers. Said Mrs Blackhorse: 'I think it is disgraceful! Since at least the year 2050 men have gone without trousers in favour of kilts and it is now the accepted and proper custom to do so. To show men wearing such ancient and sexually provocative clothing – particularly that sensuous Harris Tweed suit – is morally corrupting to the nation's youth.' Mrs Blackhorse is 115.

602. A further two girls are to be admitted to Prankton College – the former all-male public school. The first two girls – sent to the school a couple of years ago – are said to be somewhat exhausted and so need replacements. They were not replaced sooner because the boys have only just discovered that the two girls were slightly different from boys – they tired more quickly when playing rugby.

603. It was announced today that the New Forest is to be turned into a museum – although the Forest at present only consists of two trees, six blades of grass, a small pony, three hundred chemical toilets, three hundred thousand tons of rubbish and one and a half stuffed deer.

604. Mrs Bloggs-Smith was fined six thousand pounds on Thursday for talking in a public place at a rate of 95 decibels – five decibels above the permitted level. Although she explained she had to talk at this level to make herself heard above the noise of the Hippo Jets at the nearby airport, she was still ordered also to undergo an operation to reduce the risk of such offences occurring again.

NOSES
605. My young son took his nose apart this morning. He wanted to see what made it run.

606. Simon: 'You have a beautiful nose.'
    Sally: 'Yes – I picked it myself.'

NUNS
607. Two nuns were out for a drive in the country and the nun at the wheel of the car was also busily knitting.

Two policemen, seeing this, chased after the car in their patrol vehicle. Drawing level with the nuns' car, a policeman shouted from his window: 'Pull over.'

'No it's not,' shouted back one of the nuns. 'It's a woolly cover for a hassock.'

608. Inscription on a nun's tombstone: 'Returned – unopened.'

609. 'Why is Sister Mary getting so fat? I thought she was on a diet?'

'She is. But it's a seafood diet. She sees food and eats it.'

610. Not to mention the nun with a forty-six inch bust who couldn't get a bra big enough so went, weeping, to Mother Superior saying: 'My cup runneth over.'

NURSING

611. Anna Stetic – the nurse who was a real knockout.

612. Young girl: 'I'd like to see a sturgeon.'

Nurse: 'Don't you mean a surgeon?'

Young girl: 'Well, I want a contamination.'

Nurse: 'An examination?'

Young girl: 'Yes, that's right. I think I'll have to go to the fraternity ward.'

Nurse: 'Fraternity ward? Oh, you mean maternity ward, I think.'

Young girl: 'All I know is I haven't demonstrated for two months and I think I'm stagnant.'

613. Patient: 'Give me a kiss, nurse.'

Nurse: 'No.'

Patient: 'Please give me a kiss, nurse.'

Nurse: 'Certainly not!'

Patient: 'Go on, nurse, kiss me!'

Nurse: 'No, sir – and I'm not even supposed to be in bed with you.'

614. 'Nurse, is it true that uncooked eels are healthy?'

'I imagine so, sir. I've never heard any complaining.'

615. 'Give it to me straight, nurse, how long have I got?'

'It's very difficult to say, sir. But if I were you I wouldn't start reading any serials.'

616. Handsome young man, from behind a screen: 'I've taken all my clothes off, nurse. Where shall I put them?'

Young nurse: 'On top of mine.'

O

OCTOPUS

617. A man brought his pet octopus into the pub and said that he'd trained it to play any musical instrument in the whole of Britain.

At first, the pub regulars jeered, but after they had witnessed the octopus play a flute, a violin and then a saxophone, their scepticism turned into virtual amazement.

Even more difficult and complex instruments were called for – and the octopus could play them all: a harpsichord, tuba, and bassoon.

Then someone produced some bagpipes and the octopus appeared delighted – and proceeded to jump on them but did not produce any music.

'Why aren't you making music?' asked the owner of the octopus.

'Make music?' queried the octopus. 'I thought I was supposed to make love with it.'

618. Just before Christmas Fred tried to cross an octopus with a chicken – so his family could have a leg each.

OPERA

619. I knew my uncle was a true opera lover when I caught him outside the bathroom door where our beautiful au pair was having a bath. She was singing an excerpt from *Der Rosenkavalier* and my uncle didn't peer through the keyhole to look at her gorgeous naked body – but put his ear to it!

OPTICIAN
620. 'I knew you needed an optician,' said the optician to the young man.

'How did you know that?'

'Simple! You just walked in through the window.'

ORCHESTRA
621. The orchestra had just finished playing a delightful little number called 'Tuning Up', and the audience were eagerly awaiting the arrival of the world-famous conductor, Igor Driftwood.

The tension mounted as the brilliant conductor delayed his entrance until the last possible moment – then he appeared and the audience went wild with delight, clapping and jumping up and down in ecstasy at being so privileged to see such a man of sheer genius.

Igor made his way to the conductor's platform to even greater cheers. He tapped his music stand, and all was silence.

Then he looked down at the music stand and said: 'Er . . . excuse me, but what are these five lines with all the black dots and funny squiggles on them?'

ORPHANAGE
622. When asked for a donation to the local orphanage a Scotsman sent two orphans.

OWLS
623. When it is very stormy and pouring with rain owls are not very keen to go romancing. All they do is sit in the trees looking very dejected – hence their call: 'Too wet to woo; too wet to woo.'

P

PAINTING

624. Artist: 'You know, you're the first model I've ever made love to.'

Nude model: 'I don't believe you. I bet you say that to all the models you've painted. How many have you had?'

Artist: 'Well, there was a bowl of fruit, a dog, the water-mill . . .'

PANTOMIME

625. When the Smith family went to the theatre to see a pantomime they found that all the actors had died of some strange disease and so the show was put on by the ghosts of the actors instead. So it was really a phantomime.

PARROTS

626. Mrs Green had a truly remarkable parrot and when the vicar came to tea one afternoon she could not resist demonstrating to him how clever her pet was.

'If you pull this little string on its left leg Polly will sing "Abide With me",' said Mrs Green, proudly. 'And if you pull the string on its right leg it will sing "Onward Christian Soldiers".'

'How remarkable!' exclaimed the vicar. 'And what happens if you pull both strings at once?'

'Simple!' replied the parrot. 'I fall off my perch, you stupid old twit.'

627. For three years Amy Clegg's parrot had not said a single word, and eventually she became convinced it was simply a stupid parrot unable to learn to speak English.

Then one day as she was feeding it a piece of lettuce as a special treat, the parrot suddenly squawked: 'There's a maggot on it; there's a maggot on it!'

Amy Clegg was astonished: 'You can talk!' she exclaimed. 'But why haven't you spoken in all the three years that I've been keeping you?'

'Oh,' replied the parrot, 'the food has been excellent up to now.'

628. Fred at last could see a way of making a fortune. He had trained his parrot, after months of hard work, to tell jokes.

At last he felt ready to cash in on all his hard work, so he took the parrot down to his local pub.

'This is my incredible joke telling parrot,' boasted Fred.

'Go on,' jeered the pub regulars. 'We'll give you ten to one that your parrot can't tell us a joke.'

'All right,' replied Fred. 'I accept your bet.'

But try as he could, Fred was unable to make the parrot talk – let alone tell jokes.

Fred left the pub, dismally, having lost the bet. On the way home he shook the parrot and shouted: 'What do you mean by keeping quiet, you stupid bird? You made me lose a ten to one bet!'

'Ah!' squawked the parrot. 'Tomorrow you'll be able to get fifty to one.'

PARTIES
629. A lady at a cocktail party lost her handbag and she persuaded her husband to bang on a glass and call for attention and say: 'Excuse me, everyone. But my wife seems to have mislaid her handbag. It contained some very personal items in it of great sentimental value – like two hundred pounds in ten pound notes. Whoever finds it I'll give twenty pounds as a reward.'

A voice from the back of the room called: 'I'll give fifty pounds.' This was quickly followed by another voice calling: 'And if anyone brings me the bag I'll give sixty-five pounds.'

630. It seems that at cocktail parties people believe they should only open their mouths when they have nothing to say.

631. Lady Bloggis: 'We're having a party at the weekend to celebrate my daughter's coming out.'

Mavis Grunter-Tottle: 'How long was she inside – and what did she do?'

632. Algernon was boring everyone at the party. 'Yes,' he said, 'I've hunted all over India and Africa.'

'Oh,' asked the little old lady, 'what did you lose?'

633. The posh dinner party had been a great success until, over coffee, one of the guests decided to tell a long and intimately detailed blue joke.

The host of the dinner party was appalled: 'That was an outrageous joke! How dare you tell such a story before my wife!'

'I'm sorry,' replied the joke teller, 'I didn't realise your wife wanted to tell it herself!'

PERSONAL LIFE
634. I used to be engaged to a contortionist – until she broke it off.

635. I always carry some olive oil around with me in case I ever meet an olive that needs oiling.

636. You know, beneath my father's hard, cold exterior – there's a hard, cold heart.

637. I was an unwanted child – my mother wanted puppies.

638. As a small boy I felt so strongly about all the graffiti everywhere that I signed a partition.

639. I've always believed in love at first sight – ever since I looked into a mirror.

640. I was born with a silver spoon in my mouth. Once it was taken out I was all right.

641. I love kids. I used to go to school with them.

642. And my mother believed in germ-free food. She even put arsenic in my sandwiches to kill them.

643. No, that isn't my own moustache I'm wearing – my real one is in my pocket.

644. I don't smoke, don't drink and don't make passes at my girlfriend – I make my own dresses, too!

PHOTOGRAPHERS
645. The bossy, unattractive woman said to the photographer: 'Make sure your photos do me justice.'
    'Madam,' replied the photographer, 'you don't want justice – you want mercy.'

646. Herbert's wife was trying to take a photo of him so she shrieked: 'Herbert! You're not trying again. Get in focus!'

PIANISTS
647. Piano tuner: 'Good morning, sir, I've come to tune your piano.'

Mr Smith: 'But I didn't ask for a piano tuner.'
Piano tuner: 'I know, sir, but your neighbours did.'

648. I learnt to play the piano in ten easy lessons. It was the first ninety that were difficult.

649. When Cyril visited the house of his least favourite nephew he was forced to endure the latter's not very good piano playing.

After he had finished his performance the nephew asked: 'How was that?'

'You should be on TV,' replied Cyril.

'You mean I'm that good!' said the nephew, clearly delighted.

'No. But if you were on TV at least I could turn you off.'

PIGS
650. Where do wealthy pigs in America live? In styscrapers.

PLANETS
651. Two planets were talking to each other when one suddenly asked: 'Who was the star I saw you with last night?' To which the other planet replied: 'That was no star – that was my sun.'

PLASTIC SURGERY
652. A man walked into the offices of a plastic surgeon and handed over a cheque for two thousand pounds to the receptionist.

'I think there is some mistake,' said the receptionist. 'Your bill is only one thousand pounds.'

'I know, replied the man, 'but the operation was tremendously successful. The surgeon took some of the skin from my behind – where no one will ever see that it's missing – and grafted it on to my cheek and totally got rid of the large scar I used to have there.'

'So the extra thousand is for a job well done,' said the receptionist.

'Not exactly. It's a token of appreciation for all the delight I get every time my mother-in-law kisses my backside – and doesn't know it!'

POACHER

653. 'So! Caught you at last,' hissed the gamekeeper, emerging from the bushes behind a poacher.

'What do you mean?' asked the poacher.

'I saw you hastily throw that plucked duck back into the river as soon as you saw me. Look, there it is – still floating on the surface. And how do you explain all its feathers on your clothes?'

'Simple! The duck wanted to go for a swim so I'm minding its clothes.'

POKER

654. Simon: 'Claude! Stop cheating with the cards.'

Claude: 'How do you know I'm cheating?'

Simon: 'Because you're not playing the hand I dealt you.'

655. It has been said that strip poker is the only card game in which the more you lose, the more you have to show for it.

POLICE

656. The police had hired the local village hall to give a talk about crime and other problems in the neighbourhood. The police impressed on all the inhabitants of the village that their community policeman was always available to assist in the prevention of crime and nuisances like children cycling on the pavement.

Thus it was that at 1.00am the community policeman received a phone call from an elderly man. 'I can't sleep for all the noise,' he complained.

'What's causing it? Do you want me to make an arrest for breach of the peace?' asked the policeman.

'I don't know. It's two cats mating on the wall outside my house. They're making a hideous racket with all their love calls and things.'

'Cats!' exclaimed the policeman. 'Why don't you walk up to the cats, give one of them a sharp prod and tell it that he is wanted on the phone?'

'Will that make them stop?'

'It certainly stopped me,' said the community policeman, bitterly.

657. There was a serious motorway accident last night when a police van carrying three convicted thieves on their way to prison was in collision with a truck carrying a large load of cement. The prisoners escaped and the police are now looking for three hardened criminals.

658. Three tons of human hair to be made into wigs were stolen today from East Grinstead. Police are combing the area.

659. The police are also looking for a man with one eye. Typical inefficiency!

660. When thousands of bottles of perfume were stolen from a shop, the police were quick to take up the scent.

661. 'Is that the police?' asked a panic-stricken voice on the phone to the police headquarters.

'Yes, this is the police station,' replied the officer on duty.

'Oh, thank goodness! I want to report a burglar trapped in an old lady's bedroom. Please come quickly!'

'Who is that calling?' asked the policeman.

'The burglar,' replied the voice on the phone.

662. The body of a man was found today in Hyde Park. The body had been hacked into a thousand pieces and tied in a sack. Police do not yet know if it was suicide.

663. She was only a police constable's daughter, but she let the chief inspector.

664. What did the policeman say to the man with three heads?'
''Allo, 'allo, 'allo.'

665. The car was racing along the motorway at well over a hundred miles per hour when it was forced to stop by a police car.

'You were exceeding the speed limit, sir,' said a policeman. 'Would you mind blowing into this breathalyser to see if you are fit to continue your journey?'

'But I'm in a great hurry,' replied the middle-aged male driver. 'I'm perfectly fit to drive. Can't you just give me a speeding ticket and let me continue on my journey? My wife and six-year-old daughter are desperately trying to get to a party on time.'

'I'm afraid I must insist on you blowing into the breathalyser, sir,' persisted the policeman.

'But I'm perfectly capable of driving,' said the man. 'Look, try out your breathalyser on my young daughter – the thing may not even be working properly.'

The policeman agreed to this suggestion and the man's six-year-old daughter blew into the breathalyser. To the policeman's surprise, the breathalyser turned green. He admitted to the man that it must be faulty, so hurriedly wrote out a speeding ticket and let the man continue on his journey.

'I told you it would be a good idea,' said the man to his wife after they travelled a few miles.

'Yes,' agreed his wife. 'Giving our daughter a glass of rum before we set out was one of the best ideas you've had yet.'

666. 'Hello! Is that the police station?'
'Yes.'
'Have any lunatics escaped near here recently?'
'Not that I know of, sir.'
'Oh!'
'Why do you ask?'
'Someone's run off with my wife.'

667. Why did the policeman take the football away from the 22 chickens? Because he wanted to prevent fowl play.

668. Policeman: 'I'm sorry, sir, but you will have to accompany me to the station.'
Simon: 'But why?'
Policeman: 'Because it's a dark and gloomy night and I'm frightened to go there on my own.'

669. Policeman: 'So you admit to shooting your wife?'
Scotsman: 'Yes.'
Policeman: 'And you say it was because you discovered she had six lovers.'
Scotsman: 'Yes.'
Policeman: 'But if you loved your wife dearly, which you say you did, then why did you shoot her instead of the six lovers?'
Scotsman: 'I wanted to economise on bullets.'

670. The police car, its siren blaring, raced in front of a speeding car and then manoeuvred itself to force the speeding car to stop.

A heavily built policeman got out of the police car and walked over to the recalcitrant driver.

'Your name, please?' asked the policeman, taking out his notebook and pen.

'Certainly, officer,' replied the driver. 'It's Horatio Xerxes Laertes Idomeneus Aeneas Asclepius Iphicles Menoeceus Memnon Philoctetes Tyndareus Hylas.'

The policeman thought for a moment, then looked at his notebook, shook his head and said: 'I'll just give you a warning this time – don't go breaking the speed limit again.'

POLITICIANS

671. The best politicians are the honest ones – when they're bought they stay bought.

672. It is no use telling politicians to go to hell – they are trying to build it for us now.

673. A lifelong Socialist was lying, dying, on his bed when he suddenly decided to join the Tory party.

'But why?' asked his puzzled friends. 'You've been a staunch Socialist all your life.'

'Well, said the dying man, 'I'd rather it was one of them that died instead of a Socialist.'

674. A man went for a brain transplant and was offered the choice of two brains – an architect's for £10,000 and a politician's for £100,000.

'Does that mean the politician's brain is much better than the architect's?' asked the man.

'Not exactly,' replied the brain transplant salesman, 'the politician's has never been used.'

POP MUSIC

675. The new record, 'Nitrogen', is a gas.

676. The pop group threw a stick of dynamite into the audience. That really brought the house down.

677. Interviewer: 'Can you read music?'

Pop star: 'No. I can only read four letter words.'

678. Interviewer: 'Do you feel you have any obligations towards your fans?'

Pop star: 'Yes. Particularly the ones that have taken out paternity suits against me.'

679. When the female pop duo split up one of them decided to continue in the business and bought a duet-yourself-kit.

680. 'Can I sing my little number now?'
'Yes.'
'Three!'

681. Interviewer: 'What are those tiny bongos dangling from your ears?'

Pop star: 'Oh, they're just me ear drums.'

682. Interviewer: 'Can you play any musical instrument?'
Pop star: 'Yes. I'm very good on the barrel organ.'

683. Interviewer: 'I hear you have just played the Stradivarius?'

Pop star: 'Yes. That vile inn down the road.'

POPULATION EXPLOSION
684. The only reason there is a population explosion is because it is such great fun to light the fuse.

PORCUPINES
685. How do porcupines make love? Carefully . . . very carefully.

PORNOGRAPHY
686. Timothy Tittle, a rather shy middle-aged man, got lost in the back streets of Soho one day.

Suddenly a furtive looking man in a shabby raincoat slipped out of a shop doorway and sidled up to Timothy.

'Want to buy any pornographic pictures?' asked the man.

'Certainly not!' replied Timothy. 'I don't even own a pornograph.'

PREGNANCY

687. Juliet was triumphant! After five years of trying she had discovered that she was pregnant. But what was the best way of breaking this news to her husband?

She was so keen to share the news with him that she phoned him in his office and said: 'Darling, what would you say if you soon heard the patter of tiny feet around the house?'

'That it was time to move to another house,' replied her husband. 'I can't stand being in the same place as a lot of mice.'

PRESENTS

688. My husband said he wanted a big surprise for Christmas so on Christmas morning I crept up behind him and shouted 'Boo!' in his ear.

689. Algernon loved his elderly grandmother dearly and decided that for Christmas he would buy her a parrot as it would be someone for her to talk to and keep her company.

Algernon went to a pet shop and insisted that the parrot had to have a large vocabulary and he ended up paying a thousand pounds for what the pet shop owner assured him was the most talkative parrot he'd ever seen.

Algernon arranged for the parrot to be delivered to his grandmother on Christmas Eve and on Christmas Day he phoned his grandmother and asked: 'How did you like the bird I sent you?'

'It was delicious!' she replied.

690. When I won a fortune on the football pools my husband said he wanted to see the world – so I bought him an atlas.

691. When Brian was given some cuff links for Christmas he went and had his wrists pierced.

692. John: 'I don't know what to buy my girlfriend for Christmas.'
Mike: 'What about some lipstick?'
John: 'I can't buy her that – I don't know the exact size of her mouth.'

693. Penicillin – the present for the man who has everything.

694. When Mr Bloggis left the company after fifty years of loyal service his boss gave him a comb as a gift. His secretary had said it would be a good parting present.

PRISONERS
695. Eleven criminals have just escaped from a prison in Ireland by using a helicopter. Police have set up road blocks.

696. 1st prisoner: 'Why are you so unhappy?'
2nd prisoner: 'I've been sentenced to three hundred years in prison.'
1st prisoner: 'Cheer up! It could have been life.'

PROBLEMS
697. John: 'I've got a terrible problem. I've got a flat in Mayfair, an apartment in Spain, a condominium in Acapulco and I've just bought a three thousand acre estate in Surrey and my third Rolls Royce.'
Simon: 'What's wrong with that? You appear to be doing very well.'
John: 'But I only earn a hundred pounds a week . . .'

PROFESSIONS

698. A surgeon, a Field Marshal and a politician had had a very liquid lunch together and were now in a deep argument.

'A surgeon's job is the oldest profession in the world,' said the surgeon.

'What makes you say that?' asked the Field Marshal.

'Well,' replied the surgeon, 'when woman was created she was made from one of Adam's ribs and surely only a surgeon could do something like that.'

'Nonsense!' snorted the Field Marshal. 'Even before Adam and Eve there was a world and it is said that order was created out of chaos. Who else could do that but a soldier of the highest rank?'

'Ah!' said the politician. 'But who do you think created the chaos to be sorted out?'

PROFESSORS

699. A country yokel and a professor were in a train, and as it was a long journey they eventually got to talking.

'Every time you miss a riddle you give me a pound, and every time I miss one I give you a pound,' said the professor, when they had run out of the usual things to talk about.

'Ah, but you're better educated than me, so I'll give you 50p and you can give me a quid,' suggested the yokel.

The professor agreed and the yokel made up the first riddle: 'What has three legs walking and two legs flying?'

The professor didn't know, so he gave the yokel a pound. The yokel didn't know either, so he gave the professor 50p.

700. A professor dedicated his whole life to research on arachnids and their behaviour.

Eventually, after many years of patient study, he was ready to announce his findings to the world.

A special meeting of the world's top experts on arachnids was arranged, and the meeting was thrown open to the press as well – for the professor felt his findings were so amazing that the whole world should be informed.

When the audience were all seated, the professor strode into the room, ready to reveal the result of his research.

The professor placed a spider on a table in front of him and commanded the spider to walk three paces forwards. To the astonishment of the audience, the spider did as it was ordered.

'Now take three paces backwards,' commanded the professor. Again, the spider obeyed the command.

Then the professor pulled all the legs off the spider, put it back on the table and said; 'Walk forward three paces.' The spider did not move. 'Walk forward three paces,' commanded the professor, again. But still the spider did not move.

'You see,' said the professor, proudly, 'that proves that when you pull its legs off, it can't hear.'

PROTESTOR'S PLACARDS
701. 'SAVE WATER – BATH WITH A FRIEND.'

702. 'SAVE SPACE – BREED SMALLER PEOPLE.'

703. 'NO ARMS FOR VENUS DE MILO.'

PSYCHIATRIST
704. 'Why did you stop seeing the psychiatrist?'
'He kept asking personal questions.'

705. Then there was the psychiatrist who woke up one day to find himself under his bed. He decided he was a little potty.

706. 'I keep wanting to paint myself all over with gold paint.'
'Oh! You've just got a gilt complex.'

PUB

707. Algernon went into a pub and ordered seventeen pints of beer. When the barmaid gave them to him he placed them in a line and then hastily gulped down the first glass, and then the third, fifth, seventh, ninth, eleventh, thirteenth, fifteenth and seventeenth glasses and then wiped his mouth with his sleeve and got up to leave.

'Don't you want the other drinks?' asked the barmaid.

'No thanks,' replied Algernon. 'My doctor said I could only have the odd drink . . .'

Q

QUACK DOCTOR

708. 'Roll up! Roll up! Buy this miraculous cure for old age and colds. Rigor mortis can be cured! Roll up! Roll up!' called the fairground quack doctor.

He soon collected a large crowd around his stall, and the quack went on to proclaim the merits of his product. 'This miraculous mixture actually cures old age. You have only to look at me to see the proof of its power. I am over two hundred and fifty years old.'

One astonished man in the crowd turned to the quack's beautiful young assistant and said: 'Say, Miss, is what the gentleman says really true? Is he really over two hundred and fifty years old?'

'I'm afraid I can't really say,' replied the quack's assistant. 'I've only been working for him for the past ninety-three years.'

QUESTIONS

709. Clara: 'Have you heard about the silly twit who keeps saying ''no'' to questions?'

Mary: 'No.'

Clara: 'So it's you!'

710. If an artist becomes angry does he lose his tempera?

711. Did the coroner who lost his pub go on an inn quest?

712. If you suddenly heard a tap on the door would you immediately suspect a mad plumber?

713. Is a budget a baby budgerigar?

714. Is a drunken ghost a methylated spirit?

715. If a plug would not fit, would you socket?

716. What goes up bell ropes and is wrapped in a polythene bag? The lunchpack of Notre Dame.

717. What was soft, and used to sing and clean windows? Shammy Davis Jnr.

718. What is sticky and used to sing? Gluey Armstrong.

719. What is smooth, round and green and conquered the world? Alexander the Grape!

720. What is the difference between unlawful and illegal? Unlawful is against the law. Illegal is a sick bird.

721. What is the opposite of minimum? Minidad.

722. What goes in dry, comes out wet and pleases two people? A tea bag.

723. What is the difference between a barrow boy and a dachshund? The barrow boy bawls his wares on the pavement – and the other . . . has blue eyes.

724. What do you get if a cat swallows a ball of wool? Mittens.

725. What was the campaign slogan of ancient lizards millions of years ago? Things will be better come the evolution.

726. What name do spiders like best? Webster.

727. What lies at the bottom of the sea and shivers? A nervous wreck.

728. If you sat in a bucket of glue would you have a sticky end?

729. Is playing tennis courting disaster – or is it a racket?

730. 'What is fire?'
   'That is a burning question.'

731. 'Write on one of the following: Sir Thomas More, Tudor furniture, Hampton Court.'
   'No thank you. I prefer to write on paper.'

732. 'Say what you know about the French Revolution.'
   'Nothing.'

733. What weighs two tons and wears a flower behind its ear? A hippy potamus.

734. What is the difference between a buffalo and a bison? Ever tried to wash your hands in a buffalo?

735. What is brown and sounds like a bell? Dung!

736. What is one of the main causes of sleepwalking? Twin beds.

737. If a buttercup is yellow, what colour is a hiccup? Burple.

738. What does a Hindu? Lay eggs.

739. How do you stop moles digging in the garden? Hide all the shovels.

740. What are hippies for? To hang your leggies on.

741. Why do birds fly south in winter? Because it's too far to walk.

742. What is yellow and very dangerous? Shark infested custard.

743. What has got twelve legs, one eye and four tails? Three blind mice and half a kipper.

744. What has got four legs and flies? A dead horse.

745. What is it when a jester carries a nun? Virgin on the ridiculous.

746. Where do you find mangoes? Where womangoes.

747. Why does a giraffe have such a long neck? Because it can't stand the smell of its feet.

748. What do you put on a pig with a sore nose? Oinkment.

749. What goes 'putt, putt, putt, putt, putt'? A very bad golfer.

R

RACING

750. In the 1950s there was a very expensive racehorse that continually lost races which everyone had expected it to win.

'Perhaps what it needs is a bit more encouragement,' suggested the horse's owner.

So the jockey warned the horse just before the start of a major race that if it lost the race it would be the end of its racing days and the horse would have to find work elsewhere – probably on a milk round in the country.

The horse nodded at the jockey to indicate that it understood this threat, and soon the race began.

Unfortunately, this horse was soon trailing behind all the others and as the jockey urged it forward with his whip the horse turned its head and said: 'Steady on, sir. I've got to be up early in the morning.'

751. 'Are you sure you're a qualified jockey? You've put the saddle on the wrong way round.'

'How do you know which direction I'm going in?'

752. I know a man whose hobby is racing pigeons. Sometimes he's even faster than the pigeons.

RAIN

753. Colin and Mark were enjoying a quiet country stroll when suddenly they heard a noise overhead. Looking up they saw a large aeroplane and, as they watched, the door to the cargo hold burst open and hundreds of small parts intended for a Japanese motor manufacturer fell out.

'Watch out!' cried Colin. 'It's raining Datsun cogs!'

754. 'I have learnt some of white man's magic,' said the African Chief on returning to his country after a brief stay in England.

'What?' asked his brother.

'First, you must make a smooth piece of ground and get grass to grow on it. Then you carefully tend the grass. After that you place some sticks in the grass and get some men to put on all-white clothes. Two of the men have to carry pieces of wood called ''bats'' and another man has to carry a red ball. After a bit of running about between the sticks by two of the men and some throwing of the red ball, it will rain.'

755. I was once on a train with my wife and sitting next to us was a large Russian who told us that his name was Rudolf and that he was in England to attend an international conference on meteorology.

'Is that sleet or rain out there?' asked my wife.

'It looks like rain to me,' I said.

'I agree,' said the Russian.

'Well, it still looks like sleet to me,' replied my wife, who likes to argue about minor matters like the weather.

'Darling,' I responded calmly. 'It is raining. Surely you know that Rudolf the Red knows rain, dear?'

RED CORPUSCLES
756. The two red corpuscles – they loved in vein.

REINCARNATION
757. I've believed in reincarnation ever since I was a young frog.

RELIGION

758. Blessed are the pure – for they shall inhibit the Earth.

759. My father was very religious – he wouldn't work if there was a Sunday in the week.

760. The vicar was giving a Christmas party for all the children who attended Sunday school when little Melissa put up her hand and said: 'Please reverend, can I whisper something to you?'

The vicar frowned and replied: 'I'm afraid not, Melissa. We should have no secrets from one another.'

Melissa paused for a moment and then said: 'Your flies have come undone.'

761. Sunday School teacher: 'Now, Jonathan, can you tell me what sort of people go to Heaven?'

Jonathan: 'Dead ones, miss.'

762. The Sunday School teacher was talking to her class of ten-year-olds when she suddenly asked: 'Now, why do you think the Children of Israel made a Golden Calf?'

The children were silent until one spotty little boy put up his hand and said: 'Please Miss, perhaps, it was because they didn't have enough gold to make a cow.'

763. During a conversation with a kindly old priest, the young man asked: 'Is it really such a sin to sleep with a girl?'

'Oh, no,' replied the priest, 'but you young men – you don't sleep.'

764. 'Now, what have we got to do before we can get forgiveness of sin?'

'Sin.'

765. The wages of sin are high – unless you know someone who'll do it for free.

RESTAURANTS

766. Waiter: 'What would madam like for dessert?'

Customer: 'An assortment of your real cream ice cream – say, two scoops of chocolate chip, one scoop of vanilla, three scoops of banana, two scoops of strawberry and please cover the lot with thick chocolate sauce.'

Waiter: 'Certainly, madam. And would you like a few cherries on the top?'

Customer: 'No thank you. I'm on a diet.'

767. Customer: 'Waiter! Does this restaurant ever have any clean tablecloths?'

Waiter: 'I'm sorry, sir, but I've only been here for six months.'

768. Customer: 'Waiter, there's nothing worse than finding a caterpillar in my salad.'

Waiter: 'Yes there is, sir. You could have found half a caterpillar.'

769. Customer: 'Waiter!'

Waiter (walking slowly towards the customer, after having been engaged in a long conversation with three other waiters): 'Yes, sir?'

Customer: 'Are you the waiter who took my order?'

Waiter (consulting his notebook): 'Yes, sir.'

Customer: 'How are your new grandchildren?'

770. Customer: 'Waiter! How much longer do you expect me to have to wait for my poached salmon?'

Waiter: 'I'm sorry, sir, but we are trying to hurry it up for you.'

Customer: 'Then can you assure me that you're using the right bait?'

771. Waiter: 'Would you like your coffee white or black, madam?'

Customer: 'Do you have any other colours?'

772. Customer: 'Waiter! There's a worm on my plate.'
Waiter: 'That's not a worm, sir. That's your sausage.'

773. I was once in a small French restaurant when I saw a pretty young girl at the next table coughing and choking.

I quickly went to her aid and patted her back and she soon choked up a fish bone so I said: 'What's a plaice like this doing in a girl like you?'

774. Customer: 'Waiter! Will my pancakes be long?'
Waiter: 'No, madam. They will be round.'

775. A man was visiting London when he saw an advertisement for a restaurant which claimed that any dish requested could be served.

The man decided to visit this restaurant in order to test the validity of their claims. When he was seated at his table he asked the waiter for elephant ears on toast. The waiter took this order calmly, and went away into the kitchens.

A few minutes later the waiter returned and said: 'I do apologise, sir, but we've run out of bread.'

776. Customer: 'Waiter! The kitchens in this restaurant must be absolutely spotless and germ free. You've obviously got a chef who must have something of a fetish about cleanliness.'

Waiter: 'Thank you for the compliment, sir. I'm sure the chef will be pleased.'

Customer: 'It wasn't meant to be a compliment. But you've confirmed my suspicions as to why the food tastes like disinfectant.'

777. Waiter: 'Sir, would you like the chef's Surprise Pie?'
Customer: 'What's in it?'

Waiter: 'Chicken, sir.'

Customer: 'So what's the surprise?'

Waiter: 'The chef forgot to take the feathers off it.'

778. Chef: 'Sir, the waiter tells me that you don't like my famous lamb stew – yet I put my whole heart into it.'

Customer: 'That's probably what's wrong with it – you should have put lamb in it instead.'

779. The old man had never been in an expensive restaurant and it was one of the things he longed to do before he died so he carefully saved a little of his pension money each week and eventually he had enough to dine out in style.

Unfortunately, he had a rude shock when he tied his table napkin around his neck and the head waiter in the restaurant said to him: 'Would sir like a shave or a haircut?'

780. Customer: 'Waiter! Get me the chef!'

Waiter: 'Certainly, sir.'

Chef: 'You summoned me, sir?'

Customer: 'I most certainly did! This steak and kidney pie is as hard as old rocks. It's absolutely terrible!'

Chef: 'But my steak and kidney pies are delicious. I've had lots of experience making them. Indeed, I've been making them since before you were born.'

Customer: 'So why did you have to wait until now to serve them?'

781. Mr Smith was in a new restaurant that seemed to be staffed entirely by trainee waiters.

'What would you like for dessert?' asked one of the trainees.

'The cheese board, please' replied Mr Smith. So the trainee waiter scraped the cheese off it and gave him the board.

782. Customer: 'There's only one piece of meat on my plate.'
   Waiter: 'Wait a minute, sir, and I'll cut it in two.'

783. 'Waiter! This coffee tastes like mud.'
   'Well, sir, it was ground only ten minutes ago.'

784. 'Waiter! There's a dead fly in my bird's nest soup.'
   'Well, for one pound what do you expect – dead eagle?'

785. 'Waiter! There's a button in my salad.'
   'Oh! It must have come off the salad dressing.'

786. 'Waiter! Is this food pure?'
   'As pure as the girl of your dreams, sir.'
   'Oh! Then I'd rather not have it, thanks.'

787. A man was amazed to find a restaurant advertising: 'Chicken dinners – only 90p.'
   He decided to try one of these dinners so he paid his 90p and his taste buds began to anticipate the pleasant chicken dinner that was to come – until the waiter brought him a plate of corn.

788. Notice in the window of a health food restaurant: 'Our salad dinners will take your breadth away.'

789. 'Waiter! What are these coins doing in my soup?'
   'Well, sir, you said you would stop coming to this restaurant unless there was change in the meals.'

ROBBERY
790. Robber, brandishing a gun: 'Your money or your life.'
   Mr Smith: 'You'd better take my life. I'm saving my money for my old age.'

ROMANCE

791. Michael: 'I'm not feeling myself tonight.'

Mavis: 'That's good – now you can feel me for a change.'

792. The handsome young student sidled up to the young girl and asked: 'Are you going to have dinner anywhere tonight?'

The girl, who was flattered by his attentions, blushed, and replied: 'No – not that I know of.'

To which the handsome young student replied: 'What a pity – you'll be very hungry by tomorrow morning.'

793. There I was, sitting in my girlfriend's house, snuggling up to her on the sofa, when suddenly she got up and turned off all the lights. So I took the hint and went home.

794. My girlfriend says there are things a girl shouldn't do before twenty. I'm not too keen on an audience, either.

795. Pretty young girl: 'If I go up to your room do you promise to be good?'

Young man: 'Why – I promise to be FANTASTIC!'

796. Roderick was snuggling up to his girlfriend, Claudia, when she suddenly said: 'Woof! Woof!'

'What did you say that for?' asked Roderick.

'Well,' replied Claudia, 'my mother told me that you'd love me even more if I spoke in a husky voice. Isn't "woof, woof" what huskies say?'

797. The young couple had a beef stew romance – she was always beefing, and he was always stewed.

798. She started licking my cheek tenderly. I said: 'Do you love me?' She said: 'No – but I need the salt.'

799. My sister had to give up her last boyfriend because he was tall, dark, and hands . . .

800. Two young girls were talking in their office canteen when the subject, as usual, came round to discussing the men in their office.

'I wouldn't have anything to do with Graham Smith, if I were you,' said one of the girls.

'But why not?' asked her friend. 'He seems such a nice sort of man.'

'Ah! But he knows an awful lot of very dirty songs.'

'But surely he doesn't sing them in the office?' asked the friend. 'I've never heard him singing dirty songs.'

'No, perhaps not – but he certainly whistles them!'

801. 'Will you marry me?' asked the young man, getting down on his knees and offering the girl a glittering ring.

'Oooooh!' exclaimed the girl, 'are they real diamonds?'

'I hope so,' said the young man. 'Because if they aren't I've been swindled out of ten pounds.'

802. 'Darling, I want to make love before we get married,' said the girl, snuggling up to her boyfriend.

'But it won't be long until July, dear,' he replied.

'Oh!' she exclaimed enthusiastically, 'and how long will it be then?'

803. 'Will you love me always?'

'Of course – which way do you want to start with?'

804. The man kissed the girl passionately.

Girl: 'I thought a quick one before dinner meant a drink.'

805. 'He loves you terribly.'

'I keep telling *him* that.'

806. There's nothing like an expensive coat to thaw a cold shoulder.

807. Amanda: 'I had to give up Cyril.'

Amy: 'Why, what was wrong with him? He looked ravishingly handsome, was reasonably well off, and you seemed to like him a lot.'

Amanda: 'He had a number of bad habits.'

Amy: 'But we all have those.'

Amanda: 'One of them was that he always stirred his tea or coffee – even in restaurants – with his left hand.'

Amy: 'What's bad about that?'

Amanda: 'Everyone else uses a spoon.'

808. When I met my boyfriend we were rough and ready. He was rough – I was ready.

809. When we were courting we sat in the fridge because she said she wanted to slip into something cool.

810. My girlfriend used to kiss me on the lips – but it's all over now.

811. Give me your heart, darling – I'm making a monster.

812. 'Darling, what do you think of the Middle East position?'
'I don't know, I've never tried it.'

813. I met Claudia Hott-Iron yesterday – she made a great impression on me.

814. 'Darling, whisper something soft and gooey in my ear.'
'Lemon meringue pie.'

815. 'James, take off my dress. Now my bra, and now my panties . . . and if I ever catch you wearing my clothes again I'll smash your stupid face in.'

816. So I lay this beautiful young girl on the grass, ripped off her dress, tore off her stockings, grabbed hold of her panties . . . and tore out the elastic for my catapult.

817. A young girl was entertaining a rather amorous boyfriend at her home late one evening. 'If you kiss me again,' she warned, 'I'll have to call a member of my family.'

Her boyfriend kissed her passionately.

'Bro-ther,' she murmured.

818. 'If I refuse to go to bed with you, will you *really* commit suicide?'

'That has been my usual procedure, yes.'

819. Sally: 'Why are you holding your mouth like that?'

Jane: 'I've just had a mad passionate, burning kiss from my boyfriend.'

Sally: 'So what's wrong with that?'

Jane: 'He forgot to take the cigar out of his mouth first.'

820. Ethel: 'But Mr Jones can't possibly be in hospital. Only last night I saw him in a restaurant looking perfectly fit and healthy with a blonde woman.'

Sally: 'So did his wife.'

821. Hector: 'If I asked you for a kiss, what would you say?'

Gloria: 'Nothing! It's impossible for me to talk and laugh at the same time.'

822. Clarissa: 'Do you remember our holiday together last year?'

Jane: 'Yes, of course! How could I ever forget Greece?'

Clarissa: 'Do you remember, then, that boyfriend I had?'

Jane: 'Which one?'
Clarissa: 'The one I said life wasn't worth living without.'
Jane: 'Well?'
Clarissa: 'I've forgotten his name.'

823. It's easy to tell the difference between American, Chinese and Welsh girls.

American girls say: 'Gee, that was fantastic!'

Chinese girls say: 'That was wonderful. Now let's go and have a meal.'

Welsh girls say: 'Luv, the ceiling needs re-painting: do you think we can get the council to do it?'

824. Rodney: 'Is it true you're a home-loving girl?'
Sarah: 'Oh, no! I can make love anywhere.'

825. Samantha: 'Why are you moaning? You've just been given a huge diamond ring. Anyone else would be ecstatic.'

Sally: 'But the ring comes with the terrible curse of the Hyde-Whippenbrakes.'

Samantha: 'Oh – and what's the curse?'

Sally: 'With the ring comes Clyde Hyde-Whippenbrake.'

826. George: 'Sir, I don't quite know how to ask this?'
Mr Smith: 'Ask what?'
George: 'Well, I'd like your daughter for my wife.'
Mr Smith: 'Don't be ridiculous! I know we live in liberated times, but I don't think I'd like my daughter to go off with your wife.'

827. Hilary, the new groom, was in the middle of mucking out the stables when the boss's son walked in and exclaimed: 'You're pretty dirty, Hilary.'

Hilary smiled impishly and said: 'I'm even prettier when I'm clean.'

828. Her boyfriend only had one fault. He had Tarzan eyes – they swung from limb to limb.

829. 'Say when, dear.'
'After the drinks, darling.'

830. Percy: 'Something that happened to me in my child-hood may have scarred me for life. It's something you should know about before we get engaged.'
Charlotte: 'What is it? What happened?'
Percy: 'When I was about five years old I was faced with a traumatic situation. There were elephants charging in front of me. A wild lion was leaping up and down behind me. And on one side of me was a horrible black panther.'
Charlotte: 'What did you do?'
Percy: 'I had no alternative but to wait until the roundabout stopped and I could get off.'

831. Hilary: 'You're the first man I've ever said "yes" to. In fact, I've said "no" to lots and lots of men.'
Herbert: 'What were they selling?'

832. Clare: 'Darling, sometimes I think you only said you wanted to marry me because my aunt has left me half a million pounds in her will.'
Charles: 'Don't be silly, sweetheart. I'd still want to marry you – even if someone else had left you the small fortune.'

833. Gwendoline's father, a doctor, did not approve of Terence, her latest boyfriend, and had told Gwendoline what he thought of him and had also given her various other bits of advice.
Thus, when Gwendoline returned home after an evening out with Terence, her father asked her: 'Did you tell that dreadful Terence creature my opinion of him?'
Gwendoline, still thinking of earlier that evening, smiled and said; 'Yes.'

'Well,' demanded the doctor, 'what did he say?'

'You won't like it.'

'Come on!' said the doctor. 'Tell me.'

'He said he's not surprised so many of your patients ask for second opinions.'

834. The young girl arrived home late from an evening out with her boyfriend. As she stormed into her flat and slammed the door her flatmate came out of her bedroom to see what all the noise was about.

'Oh!' exclaimed the girl. 'Berkeley really is the limit! I had to slap his face several times this evening!'

'Why, what did he do?' asked her flatmate, eagerly.

'Nothing, unfortunately,' muttered the pretty young girl. 'I had to slap his face to see if he was awake.'

835. Annette: 'Why are you marrying that hideously ugly old man? I know he's rich, but he's at least sixty years older than you.'

Angela: 'It's because he's got a very strong will – made out to me.'

836. A married man fell in love with a mermaid and everything went well with their affair until his wife began to smell something fishy . . .

837. Eighteen-year-old son: 'Dad?'

Father: 'Yes, son?'

Eighteen-year-old son: 'Did you ever make love when you were my age?'

Father: 'Yes, son. And let it be a horrible warning to you.'

Eighteen-year-old son: 'Why, what happened?'

Father: 'I ended up marrying your mother.'

838. Julia, snuggling up to Derek on the sofa: 'Dearest, you're a man in a million.'

'What!' shrieked Derek, pushing Julia away from him. 'There have been *that* many others!'

839. Claudia likes to bring out the animal in her wealthy new boyfriend – like mink, musquash . . .

840. Simon and Sarah were snuggled up on the sofa when Simon said: 'You know, I've been thinking. For the past few years I've been content just living on my own. But now I feel the need for a faithful companion. Someone who will always be there when I come home. Someone who will look at me with devotion in their eyes. Someone who . . .'

Sarah interrupted him: 'That's a great idea! Shall we go together to the pet shop and I'll help you choose the puppy?'

841. David: 'Last night I invited my girlfriend up to my flat for a surprise meal.'

Derek: 'Isn't she that gorgeous Chinese girl?'

David: 'Yes. So I thought I'd demonstrate my culinary arts and cook her something Chinese – but when I asked how she'd like her rice, boiled or fried, she replied ''Thrown''.'

842. Simon had been separated from his girlfriend for a week since he went to live and work in a neighbouring village. There was no bus service between the two villages, and – not having a car – the only way they could meet was to walk the three miles between their villages.

Thus, Simon wrote to his girlfriend:

'My dearest, darling Sally,

My heart pounds whenever I think of you. I love you more than mere words can tell. I would plunge to the depths of the deepest ocean, climb the highest mountain, cross the most desolate desert, take a rocket to the moon, or brave the coldest wastes of the Arctic Circle just for a glimpse of your adorable smile. I love you with all my heart, Simon.

P.S. I'll come over and see you Sunday – if it's not raining.'

843. He used to go out with a girl called Ruth. Then she left him, so he became ruthless.

844. Man, snuggling up to girl: 'Am I the first man you ever made love to?'

Girl, pushing man back and looking at him carefully: 'You might be – your face looks familiar.'

845. Masochist: 'Hit me!'

Sadist: 'No.'

S

SALESMEN

846. John was at a cocktail party where he was boasting about his latest sales success. 'And do you know how much I sold?' he asked his bored victim.

'Probably about half,' replied the bored fellow.

'Half? What do you mean by half?' asked John.

'Half of what you will tell me you sold.'

847. The little old lady was busy dusting with her feather duster in her little old cottage deep in the countryside when there was a knock on the door.

'Good morning, madam,' said the suave young man when she opened the door, and he pushed his way into the house saying: 'What a lovely house but I'm sure you'll be interested in what I can offer you.'

'But . . .' started the old woman, before being interrupted by the young man who had by now pulled a large bag of soot, dust and other small items of rubbish from his pocket and was sprinkling them all over the carpet.

'Don't worry,' said the young man, 'what I have in my car outside will soon remove all this rubbish, dust and soot and I'll even demonstrate by cleaning your other rooms, too. So effective is my new machine that it will even suck out ground-in dust and dirt like this' and he used his heel to drive into the pile of the carpet some of the soot.

'But . . .' tried the old lady, again, but to no avail as the young man had rapidly gone out of the front door and soon reappeared with a vacuum cleaner.

'Now, where can I plug this in?' he asked.

'Probably the next village, about ten miles away,' replied the old lady. 'The electricity supply hasn't reached here yet!'

848. At an international sales exhibition, one British salesman turned to another and asked: 'How are you faring so far today?'

'Quite well,' replied the other salesman. 'I've picked up lots of useful information, followed up a number of promising leads, renewed relationships with a number of potential customers and made a lot of valuable new contacts.'

'So have I,' responded the first salesman. 'I haven't sold anything yet, either.'

SCHOOL

849. Teacher: 'You've put your shoes on the wrong feet.'
Small boy: 'But these are the only feet I've got.'

850. Teacher: 'If I were to ask you to add 9,731 to 232 and then halve it, what do you think you would get?'
Simon: 'The wrong answer, sir.'

851. Teacher: 'Where are you from?'
New pupil: 'Devon, miss.'
Teacher: 'Which part?'
New pupil: 'All of me, miss.'

852. Teacher: 'Sally, can you name an animal that lives in Australia?'
Sally: 'A kangaroo, miss.'
Teacher: 'That's good. Can you tell me the name of another animal that lives in Australia?'
Sally: 'Another kangaroo, miss.'

853. Teacher: 'Now tell me, Millicent, where were English monarchs usually crowned?'
Millicent: 'On their heads, miss.'

854. Teacher: 'Can anyone tell me what family the crocodile belongs to?'

Samantha: 'I'm sorry, miss, but nobody we know owns one.'

855. Headmaster: 'Why are you late for school?'

Pupil: 'I'm sorry, sir. But on the way I tripped and sprained my ankle.'

Headmaster: 'That's a lame excuse.'

856. Teacher: 'Now, Cressida, can you tell me what a cannibal is?'

Cressida: 'No, miss.'

Teacher: 'Well, if you ate your mother and father, what would you be?'

Cressida: 'An orphan, miss.'

857. English teacher: 'I'm sure if John Milton were with us today we'd still regard him as an exceptional man.'

Pupil: 'Yes, sir. Especially as he'd be nearly four hundred years old.'

858. Teacher: 'Sarah, if it takes ten men two days to dig up a large garden, how long would it take five men to dig up the same garden?'

Sarah: 'No time at all, miss. The first ten men have already dug it up.'

859. 'Get up,' shouted Albert's mother. 'You'll be late for school.'

'But I don't want to go,' protested Albert. 'All the kids are horrible, the teachers are terrible, and it's all extremely boring. I want to stay home.'

'But,' replied Albert's mother, 'you're forty-three and the headmaster of the school.'

860. Teacher, 'Tell me, Amber, is the world flat or is it round?'

Amber: 'Neither, miss. My Mum keeps telling me it's crooked.'

861. Small boy: 'Please, miss, would you be angry and tell me off for something I didn't do?'

Teacher: 'No, of course not.'

Small boy: 'Oh, good! Then I can tell you I haven't done my homework.'

862. Teacher: 'I'll give this shiny apple to anyone who can tell me who was the greatest man in the world.'

Little David Cohen put his hand up and said: 'It was Jesus, miss.'

Teacher: 'Well done, David – you're perfectly right. But I always thought you were Jewish?'

David: 'So I am, miss. And *you* know and *I* know it was really Moses who was the greatest man in the world – but business is business.'

863. 'What are you making, Tommy?' asked the woodwork teacher.

'A portable,' replied the small boy.

'A portable what?'

'I don't yet know, sir. I've only made the handle.'

864. 'Mummy, teacher was asking me today if I have any brothers and sisters who will be coming to school.'

'That's nice of her to take such an interest, dear. What did she say when you told her you are an only child?'

'She just said: "Thank goodness!" '

865. A teacher warned her pupils to wrap up warm against the cold winter, and to show how important this was she told them of the true story of her little brother who took his sledge out in the snow one day. Unfortunately, her brother hadn't been wrapped up properly and he caught pneumonia and died a few days later.

There was silence in the classroom for a few moments, then a small voice at the back said: 'Please Miss, what happened to his sledge?'

866. Pupil: 'Can I have a cigarette?'
Teacher: 'Good heavens! No, certainly not! Do you want to get me into trouble?'
Pupil: 'Well, all right then, Miss. But I'd rather have a cigarette.'

867. Teacher: 'Can you name three members of the cat family?'
Pupil: 'Daddy cat, mummy cat and baby cat.'

868. Teacher: 'Can anyone tell me what Picasso and Braque have in common?'
Simon: 'They are both dead, sir.'

869. Teacher: 'What cake do you dislike the most?'
Young pupil: 'A cake of soap.'

870. Teacher: 'Everything you do is wrong. How can you expect to get a job when you leave school if everything you do is inaccurate?'
Pupil: 'Well, sir! I'm going to be a TV weatherman.'

871. Teacher: 'Mavis, can you tell me which month is the shortest?'
Mavis: 'It's May, miss.'
Teacher: 'No, it isn't. The shortest month is February.'
Mavis: 'But, miss, February has eight letters in it while May only has three!'

872. Teacher: 'Lionel, can you tell me a word with four letters, that ends in 'k' and is another word for intercourse?'
Lionel: 'Really, sir! How could you ask such a question?

You just want to get me expelled by saying a swear word!'

Teacher: 'Swear word? What swear word? The word I was looking for is "talk"!'

873. A little boy and a little girl were walking home from school.

'Guess what I found behind the radiator in our class?' asked the little boy.

'What?' inquired the little girl.

'I found a contraceptive behind the radiator.'

'What's a radiator?'

874. Chemistry teacher: 'What can you tell me about nitrates?'

Pupil: 'Well sir . . . er . . . they're a lot dearer than day-rates.'

875. A middle-aged woman was on her way to the shops when she saw a small boy leaning against a wall, smoking a cigar and swigging a bottle of whisky. The woman was appalled by this and rushed over to the boy and demanded: 'Why aren't you at school at this time of day?'

'At school?' queried the boy, taking another swig at the bottle. 'Hell, lady, I'm only four years old!'

SCHOOL REPORTS
876. Music: Has a very musical ear, which gives B flat when twisted.

877. English: Knott upp two hiz bezt werk. Iz badd att speling annd mayks litle efort.

878. Science: I am enclosing the bill for one science laboratory.

879. Mathematics: 3 and easy, but 2 easily distracted 4 various reasons.

880. Religious Knowledge: He will definitely go to Hell.

881. History: He likes dates – and figs. Knows much about the Cabinet – much to their horror.

SCHOOL REUNIONS

882. It was the class reunion and Derek went up to a man and said: 'I almost didn't recognise you. The last time I saw you I thought you looked quite ill: you were very pale and thin and your hair seemed to be receding. Now you look healthy, fit and have grown a moustache. Are you on a new diet or something Jeremy?'

'I'm not Jeremy.'

'Oh!' said Derek. 'Then you've changed your name to go with your new image?'

883. It was ten years since Philip and Andrew had left school and in those ten years they had not met.

Then, at the school reunion dinner, they sat next to each other.

'How has life treated you since leaving school?' asked Andrew.

'Oh, I've had my ups and downs. But now I'm doing quite well as an estate agent. We've got offices in fifteen towns and villages in the area and hope to open a London branch next year.'

'That sounds good,' replied Andrew.

'And how have you done since leaving school?' asked Philip.

'Not so good,' said Andrew. 'You know when I was at school I fancied Fiona? Well, I married her soon after school – but within three months of marriage she left me for another man. Then my second wife ran off with her girlfriend. The new house I bought by the sea was a bit too near it – within a year after buying it the cliff it was on fell into the sea, taking the house and all my possessions with it. And you probably saw that I walk with a limp. That's the result of falling out of my canoe and being crushed against a weir. And today didn't start too well, either. My dog was run over and killed by a bus and my motorcycle was set on fire by vandals.'

'But, if you don't mind me asking,' said Philip, 'What do you do for a living?'

'Oh!' replied Andrew, 'I sell good luck charms.'

SEA
884. Why did the sea roar?
Because it discovered crabs in its bed.

885. Young man: 'Sir, your daughter was struggling in the sea so I pulled her out and resuscitated her.'
Retired colonel: 'Then, by George, you'll marry her!'

SÉANCE
886. The little girl was taken by her father to a séance which was being held at the home of a friend of his who worked in the same factory.

When they arrived at the house the séance had just started and the medium asked the little girl if there was anyone she would like to speak to. 'I'd very much like to talk to my old grandmother,' replied the little girl in a soft voice.

'Certainly, my dear,' said the medium, and shortly afterwards went into a trance. Suddenly the medium began to talk in a strange voice – the voice saying: 'This is your old grandmother speaking from Heaven – a glorious place high in the skies. Would you like to ask me anything, my child?'

'Yes, grandmother,' said the little girl. 'Why are you speaking from Heaven when you're not even dead yet?'

SECRETARIES

887. Mr Smith's wife decided to make an unexpected visit to her husband's office in order to take a look at his new secretary.

'You liar!' hissed Mrs Smith to her husband. 'You told me that your new secretary was very efficient and capable but that she looked like a horrible old hag. But I've just seen her and she's about eighteen years old, extremely pretty and . . .'

'But she's *not* my secretary,' interrupted Mr Smith, who had been thinking very rapidly. 'My secretary is ill today and so sent her grand-daughter to help out instead.'

888. Office manager: 'Clara, you've been seen kissing a number of the male clerks in the stationery cupboard; have been observed cuddling the messenger boy; and today I find you canoodling with a trainee accountant. What sort of a reference can I possibly give you after that sort of behaviour?'

Trainee secretary: 'Perhaps you could say that while I was training I tried my best to please as many people as possible in the office.'

889. Boss: 'Did you take any messages while I was out?'

Young secretary: 'No. Are any of them missing?'

890. Boss: 'Please file these letters immediately.'

New secretary: 'But filing them will take ages. Couldn't I just trim them with a small pair of scissors instead?'

891. New secretary: 'You seem to know your way around very well. How long have you worked here?'

Secretary: 'Ever since the boss told me he'd sack me if I didn't.'

892. The secretary heard footsteps and hastily put down the phone as her boss came into her office.

'How many times must I tell you?' thundered her boss. 'You must *not* use the office phones for personal calls.'

'But I wasn't,' protested the secretary. 'It was a business call.'

'Then,' responded her boss, 'you might like to tell me which person it is that this company does business with who is called ''darling sweetheart''!'

893. Boss: 'You've had days off already this month for your father-in-law's funeral, your son's christening, your daughter's illness, and your brother-in-law's wedding – why on earth do you want another day off work tomorrow?'

Secretary: 'I'm getting married.'

894. Charles: 'I hear your new secretary is fantastic to look at – but rather dim. Is that right?'

Claude: 'Well, she did spend all afternoon trying to phone a VAT number.'

895. The young girl applied to be an executive secretary and all went well at her job interview until she asked: 'And how much will I be paid?'

'You will be paid what you are worth,' said the personnel manager with a smile.

'Huh!' replied the girl, getting up and walking towards the door. 'I couldn't possibly work for as little as that!'

SECRETS
896. My wife thinks that a secret is something you tell one person at a time.

SERVANTS

897. The new maid had just arrived to work at the magnificent stately pile in which live the Duke and Duchess.

'One thing is very important,' said the Duchess, imperiously, 'and that is that my husband and I always have breakfast at eight sharp.'

The new maid nodded her head in agreement and said: 'Sounds fine by me, Duchess. If I should sleep late, please feel free to start without me. I never eat much breakfast anyway.'

898. The mother of one of the servants came storming into the lord's manor, demanding to see the lord.

'What is it you want?' asked the lord, when the angry woman was brought before him.

'It's about my daughter, Jenny – she works here,' said the woman. 'You've got her pregnant!'

'Don't worry,' replied the lord. 'If she really *is* pregnant then I'll give you some money – and when the little one comes along I'll set up a trust fund with at least half a million. Does that seem fair?'

'You're very kind,' agreed the woman, 'but if it doesn't happen – will you give her another chance?'

SEX

899. In the East End of London people learn about life very quickly.

Two boys were playing in the street when they saw a friend peering through a window into a house.

'Quick!' he said. 'There's a man and a woman fighting in bed.'

One of the other boys, aged about six, looked and said: 'They're not fighting – they're making love.'

The third little boy had a look, too, and said: 'Yes – and badly.'

900. Brian's mother and father had told him about the facts of life, but when it came to telling their younger son, only seven years old, they were too embarrassed.

'Brian, will you tell John about the birds and the bees?' pleaded Brian's father.

Brian agreed and that night Brian asked John: 'Do you know what mum and dad do at night in bed?'

'Of course I know,' replied John.

'Well,' said Brian, 'it's the same with birds and bees.'

901. How do you tell the sex of a hormone? Take its genes off.

902. 'It was the bells that killed my husband,' sobbed the nineteen-year-old girl at the funeral of her ninety-eight-year-old husband.

'All week,' she continued, 'he would save up his strength so that we could make love on a Sunday morning. He liked to do it to the rhythm of the church bells. If that stupid ice cream van hadn't gone past chiming its stupid tune I'm sure he would still be here today.'

903. 'Do you ever talk to your wife when making love?'
   'Only if she telephones.'

904. A young man was loudly lamenting to everyone in the bar that his doctor had ordered him to give up half his sex life.

'Which half are you going to give up?' asked a bored listener. 'Talking about it – or thinking about it?'

905. Today all the young girls are out all night sowing their wild oats – and in the morning you can find them praying for a crop failure.

906. A gamekeeper was walking across a clearing when he saw a nude young woman walking towards him.

'Are you game?' he asked.
'Yes,' she replied.
So he shot her.

SHOPPING

907. Customer: 'Can I have half a pound of mixed nuts, please?'

Shop assistant: 'Certainly, madam.'

Customer: 'And please make sure there are not too many coconuts.'

908. Customer: 'Do you have any crocodile shoes?'

Shoe shop assistant: 'Certainly, madam. What size feet do your crocodiles have?'

909. The newly opened shopping centre has three tailors – right next to each other. Coincidentally, all three tailors are named Jacob Silverstein.

The first tailor has a sign over his shop which proclaims: 'Jacob Silverstein – High Class Tailor.'

The second tailor has a sign saying: 'Silverstein – the tailor of distinction.'

The third tailor has a smaller notice above his shop, but it says: 'Silverstein's Tailors – Main Entrance.'

910. Jacob was dying and the family gathered around his bedside.

'Mama,' he whispered.

'I'm here, Jacob,' she replied.

'Rachel,' he sighed.

'I'm here, Papa.'

'Isaac!'

'I'm here, Papa.'

'Levi?' he coughed.

'I'm here, too, Papa.'

'Then,' he wheezed, 'who the hell is minding the shop?'

911. The man was in the Army Surplus store browsing around when a shop assistant came up to him and asked: 'Can I help you sir?'

'No thanks,' replied the man. 'I think I've found what I want.' And he selected an army penknife. 'It's a gift for my wife,' he explained.

'Is it going to be a surprise?' asked the shop assistant. 'If so, we can gift wrap it for you.'

'Yes, please,' said the man. 'That way it will be a double surprise – she's expecting a diamond bracelet.'

912. Mrs Bloggis: 'I'd like some nuts, please.'
Shop assistant: 'Certainly, madam. What sort?'
Mrs Bloggis: 'Cashew.'
Shop assistant: 'Bless you! Now what nuts would you like, madam?'

913. Shopping in a supermarket is a very educational process. Before I went there I didn't know that fish had ten fingers.

914. The little girl had been taken to the supermarket by her mother but had somehow managed to get lost near the tinned food section.

'Excuse me,' the little girl asked another customer. 'Have you seen a mother walking along pushing a shopping trolley without a girl like me?'

SKUNKS
915. Tom: 'How many skunks do you need to make a really great stink?'
John: 'Quite a phew.'

SPACE SCIENTISTS
916. It was the annual meeting of the international brotherhood of space scientists in 2097.

'We are preparing to send a rocket to Pluto,' announced the Americans, proudly. 'It will have six men aboard and will stay on Pluto for a whole month before making the long trip back to Earth.'

'That's nothing!' scoffed the Russians. 'We are almost ready to launch our spaceship containing two hundred men and women to start the first colony on Uranus.'

'Our country can beat you both,' said the Irish scientist. 'We are going to send a rocket straight to the Sun.'

'Don't be silly,' said the American and Russian scientists, 'the rocket will melt before it gets there.'

'No it won't,' replied the Irish scientist. 'We're sending it up at night.'

SPEECHES
917. 'Why did you walk out in the middle of my speech?' demanded the company Chairman of one of his senior executives. 'It was a very important meeting of shareholders and you chose the most crucial moment to walk out when I had been speaking for only forty-five minutes.'

'I'm sorry, sir,' replied the senior executive, 'but it wasn't anything personal. I was just sleepwalking.'

918. A business executive had to make a speech at an important meeting attended by his business associates. He couldn't think of anything interesting to talk about, so in the end he decided to talk about sex.

When he arrived home his wife asked him how his speech had gone. He replied that it had been a huge success.

'But what did you talk about?'

The man thought for a few seconds, then replied: 'Oh, sailing.'

The following week one of the man's business colleagues approached the man's wife at a cocktail party and commented: 'That was a marvellous speech your husband made last week.'

'I know,' replied the wife. 'It's amazing. He's only tried it twice. The first time his hat blew off and the second time he was sea-sick.'

919. The rather conceited politician was giving his usual long, boring, speech – when one of his suffering audience could stand it no longer.

As a bullet whistled past the speaker's ear, the conceited speaker said: 'I see my speech is so moving that a man in the front row was moved to commit suicide. Unfortunately, he needs an optician as the bullet just missed my ear.'

SPIES

920. In the days of the Cold War Boris Goronovitch, the Russian sportsman and top secret agent, arrived in Swansea. His highly secret assignment was to contact Jones at the address he had been given. But the address turned out to be a large block of flats, in which five men, all named Jones, happened to live.

Taking a chance, Boris Goronovitch knocked on the door of the Jones on the first floor. As the door opened, Boris whispered: 'The wombats are migrating early this year.'

'Oh, no!' came a voice from within. 'I'm Jones the Milk, the local milkman. You want Jones the Spy – two floors up. Good-bye!'

921. A British diplomat in Moscow was attending a dinner party at the Kremlin, and much to his enjoyment he found himself seated next to a beautiful young woman.

During the course of the meal the diplomat dropped his handkerchief, and gently stroked the ankle of the young woman as he picked it up. But this brought no response.

The diplomat soon dropped a fork, and gently patted the woman's knee when he picked up the fork. But the woman still remained silent.

As he dropped his knife to the floor, the diplomat noticed the young woman scribbling hastily on the back of a menu. She handed him what she had written and the diplomat was somewhat surprised to read: 'When you reach your destination show no astonishment. Roger Barrington-Smythe, MI5.'

SPORTS AND SOCIAL CLUB
922. Gerald: 'I understand the sports and social club is looking for a treasurer.'

Edwin: 'That's right.'

Gerald: 'But I thought the sports and social club only hired a treasurer a few months ago?'

Edwin: 'They did. That's the treasurer they are looking for.'

STRIPPER
923. 'Boy, you should have seen the stripper at the Club last night. That unbelievable 55–26–37 figure . . .'

'What kind of a dance did she do?'

'Well, she didn't actually dance – it was more like she crawled around on stage and tried to stand up.'

STUDENTS
924. One female student to another. 'The new tutor is gorgeous, isn't he. He dresses so well.'

Second girl: 'Yes, and so quickly, too!'

925. 1st student: 'Why are you saving all those old magazines?'

2nd student: 'Because I qualify as a doctor in five years' time and I'll need something suitable for my waiting room.'

SWIMMING
926. I learned to swim at a very early age. When I was three my parents used to row me out to sea in a little boat until they got about a mile or so away from the shore – then I had to swim back. I quite liked the swim – it was getting out of the sack that was difficult.

T

TECHNOLOGY

927. Clarence: 'What would you like for Christmas?'

Clara: 'A video cassette recorder. But I know we can't afford one.'

Clarence: 'That's all right. I'll sell something in order to get enough money for one.'

Clara: 'What will you sell?'

Clarence: 'The television set.'

928. You know my computerised, digital, rustproof, elephant proof, shockproof, waterproof watch? Well, it's just caught fire.

929. Modern technology is wonderful! In the bad old days we always used to burn the toast every breakfast time – now we can buy the latest automatic toaster and the burnt toast pops up automatically.

TELEPHONE

930. Bell invented the telephone, but he found it was useless until he invented the second telephone. This was fine, until he invented the third telephone, phoned the second, and found it engaged.

TELEVISION

931. The problem with American television detective/police series is not deciding which to watch but deciding which is which.

932. 'Excuse me, madam, we are doing a survey. Can you tell me what you think of sex on the television?'
  'Very uncomfortable.'

THEATRE
933. Simon: 'I took my wife to the theatre last night – but we only saw the first Act and then had to leave.'
  Sally: 'Why was that?'
  Simon: 'Well, on the programme it said: "Act Two: Two days later" – and we couldn't stay in the theatre that long.'

934. The wealthy man booked the royal box at the London theatre so that he could take his pet elephant with him to watch a play.
  Everyone was surprised at how well the elephant behaved and the manager of the theatre commented on this: 'Your elephant certainly seemed to enjoy himself. I could see him paying close attention to everything. I must say I was somewhat surprised that he should like the play so much.'
  'So was I,' replied the wealthy man. 'When he read the book the play was based on he didn't like it at all.'

TIGER
935. Then there was the tiger who caught measles and became so spotty the other tigers banished him to the leopard colony.

TOASTER
936. Jeffrey: 'We have a Red Indian toaster at home.'
  Jeremy: 'What's a Red Indian toaster?'

Jeffrey: 'Instead of the toast popping up it sends up smoke signals.'

TOMBSTONE
937. When Sally saw the tombstone with the inscription: 'Here lies the body of a politician and an honest man' she wondered how they managed to get two people into the same grave.

TRAVEL
938. Cashier at car wash: 'Hello! Seeing an Irishman like you this morning has really cheered me up.'

Irishman: 'How did you know I was Irish?'

Cashier at car wash: 'Well, we don't get many people riding motorcycles in here.'

939. If a broad bean is a double-decker bus and a runner bean is a single-decker bus – then what is a pea? A relief.

940. What did the traffic lights say to the sports car? Don't look now, I'm changing.

941. Customer: 'A return ticket, please.'
Airline reservations clerk: 'Where to, sir?'
Customer: 'Back here, please.'

942. Very rich (but old) husband: 'I'm going to fire my pilot. He nearly killed me again today with his dreadful flying.'

Very young (but bored) wife: 'But, darling, can't you give him one last chance?'

943. Air traffic controller: 'What is your height and position?'
Pilot: 'I'm about five feet ten inches tall and I'm sitting in the pilot's seat.'

944. Pilot: 'What's happened to all my controls? Some idiot has daubed black and white paint all over them!'

Trainee pilot: 'But you just told me to *check* the instrument panel, sir.'

945. The aeroplane was so old it even had an outside lavatory.

946. The bearded man stuck a gun in the pilot's back and hissed: 'Take me to London.'

Pilot: 'But we're supposed to be going to London, anyway.'

Bearded man: 'I know. But I've been hi-jacked to Cuba twice before, so this time I'm taking no chances.'

947. As the train thundered along, the man turned to the woman in the otherwise deserted compartment and said: 'Would you let me kiss you for five pounds?'

'Certainly not!' retorted the woman.

The man returned to his newspaper.

A few minutes later, the man asked: 'Would you let me kiss you for a thousand pounds?'

'Yes,' replied the woman, after a brief pause.

A few minutes later the man asked: 'Would you let me kiss you for ten pounds?'

'Certainly not!' exclaimed the woman. 'What kind of a woman do you think I am?'

'We've already established that. Now we're just haggling over the price.'

948. While travelling in a sleeping compartment in a train, the man in the top bunk was woken up by someone tapping from below. 'Hello?' he said.

'Are you awake?' asked a female voice from below.

'Yes.'

'It's terribly cold down here. I wonder if you would mind letting me have an extra blanket.'

'I've got a better idea,' replied the man. 'Let's pretend we are married.'

'That's a lovely idea!' giggled the woman.

'Right,' said the man, 'now get your own damn blanket!'

949. It was the first scheduled passenger flight to the Moon. The two hundred passengers fastened their seat belts and the gigantic spaceship nosed its way up through the clouds towards its far off destination.

The passengers could hear the soft throbbing of the powerful engines and settled back in their comfortably padded seats to enjoy the journey.

Then a voice broke in on the passengers and said: 'Good morning, ladies and gentlemen! And a very warm welcome to Mini-Moon Trips – and our first scheduled passenger flight to the Moon. It may interest you to know that this brilliantly constructed spaceship has been checked and doubled checked; and to eliminate the possibility of any human errors the spaceship is completely crewed by robots; so rest assured, ladies and gentlemen, nothing at all can go wrong . . . can go wrong . . . can go wrong . . .'

TURTLES
950. Two small crabs were walking along the beach in Malaysia when one said to the other: 'I can't remember who my mother is.'

'That's terrible,' said the other crab. 'Maybe you should go and ask a turtle – they have tremendous memories.'

'Oh,' replied the first crab. 'I didn't know turtles had such good memories.'

'Of course,' commented the other crab. 'Haven't you heard of turtle recall?'

U

UNIVERSITY

951. 'Now,' said the lecturer, 'I shall be talking today about the heart, lungs, liver . . .'

'Oh dear,' murmured one of the students, 'I just can't stand organ recitals.'

952. The female student went to the end of term ball taking two handkerchiefs with her, as she had a cold. One handkerchief she put in her handbag and the other she tucked down the front of her dress.

During the course of the evening she finished using the first and so tried to retrieve the second, but she couldn't find it.

The University's Chancellor, sitting nearby and watching her with interest, was amazed to hear her remark: 'I could have sworn I had two when I came in.'

UPPER CRUST

953. Someone once defined the upper crust as being a half-baked group of crumbs supported by a lot of dough.

V

VANITY

954. John: 'Would you say that I am very vain?'

Sarah: 'No, of course not. Why?'

John: 'Well, other men as handsome, intelligent and sexy as me usually are very vain.'

955. Sally: 'Whenever I see a mirror I can never resist looking into it for at least a few minutes to admire my flawless complexion. Do you think that's vanity?'

Samantha: 'No. More like imagination.'

956. Tim: 'What's your New Year's Resolution?'

Frank: 'To be much less conceited.'

Tim: 'Will that be difficult to maintain for a year?'

Frank: 'Not for someone as clever and intelligent as me.'

VICARS

957. In our small village the vicar has asked us for money for repairs to the church, a new church hall, new hymn books and so many other causes that we're now known not as his flock, but as his fleeced.

958. A very attractive young girl was about to enter the Church in a topless dress when the vicar ran towards her.

'I'm very sorry, madam,' said the vicar, 'but I cannot possibly allow you to go into Church like that.'

'But I have a divine right,' protested the young girl.

'Yes,' agreed the vicar, 'and you have a divine left, too, but I still cannot let you into my Church like that.'

959. A vicar called Mark was closing the Church doors after an evening service when he heard a strange voice call: 'Mark! Mark!'

He looked outside the Church, but could find no one calling his name. Then he looked inside the Church, but although the voice still called 'Mark! Mark' the poor clergyman could not find where the sounds were coming from.

Finally, he rushed to the altar, thinking it must be God calling him. But when he got there all he found was a dog with a hare lip.

960. The vicar was passing the local pond when he heard a little voice. He looked around, but could see no one. Still the voice continued. Then he saw a frog sitting near the edge of the pond. The frog told the vicar that it had been turned into a frog by a wicked witch. The vicar was naturally horrified and asked the frog what he could do to help. The frog said that he was really a sixteen-year-old boy and all the vicar had to do to remove the witch's spell was to take him home and put him in the vicar's nice warm bed. And that, m'lud, concludes the evidence for the defence.

961. The vicar was explaining the difference between knowledge and faith to his congregation.

'In the front row,' he said, 'we have Mr Heather with his wife and three children. Now, she knows they are her children – that's knowledge. He believes they are his children – that's faith.'

962. Vicar: 'You know, I pray for you every night.'

Young woman: 'Well, there's really no need – I *am* on the phone.'

W

WAGES
963. Twenty years ago I used to dream about the time when I would be living in fantastic luxury on the same wages that are now keeping me below the poverty line.

WAR BABY
964. My husband was a war baby. When he was born his parents took one look at him and started fighting.

WATER SKIER
965. An Irishman bought a pair of water skis – now he spends all his time looking for water with a slope.

WEATHER
966. Resident of Barbados: 'In Barbados we always have fantastic weather.'

Visiting English woman: 'Then how on earth do you start a conversation with a stranger?'

967. Sally: 'How did you find the weather on holiday?'
Debbie: 'I just went outside and there it was.'

WEDDING ANNIVERSARY
968. Mr and Mrs Smith had been married fifty years but had

always had many friends and so not missed never having any children.

The Golden Wedding Anniversary celebrations had been very successful and so it was a slightly drunk Mr and Mrs Smith who went to bed shortly after the last guest had left.

In bed, Mrs Smith lay and looked at the ceiling as she said: 'You know, all this festivity brings back memories of our wedding.'

'And our honeymoon,' said Mr Smith.

'Yes. It was a pity we were both so young and inexperienced then. Sixteen really was too young for people in those days to have got married. Of course, young people today know far more about the facts of life than we ever did when we first got married.'

'I know, dear,' replied Mr Smith. 'Young people today wouldn't have had the same difficulties we had on our wedding night.'

'Darling,' said Mrs Smith, 'would you like to try for a second time?'

WEDDINGS

969. Henry: 'My girlfriend and I want to get married in church. But do you approve of sex before the marriage service?'

Clergyman: 'If it delays the service – no!'

970. I once knew a very sporting country gentleman who put a silencer in his shotgun because he wanted his daughter to have a quiet wedding.

971. If the bride wears white for her wedding as a symbol of purity and joy – then why does the groom always wear the opposite, black?

972. I recently went to a wedding which was the result of a love match pure and simple: the bride was pure and the groom was simple.

WEEVILS
973. The public health inspector was sent to Merseyside to look for the destructive beetle of the Curculionidae family known as the weevil.

The public health inspector dutifully searched in Liverpool and the surrounding areas – and even looked in the sea – but he finally had to report back to his boss in Liverpool: 'Here no weevil, sea no weevil, Speke no weevil.'

WHALES
974. Where do you weigh whales? At a whale weigh station.

WILLS
975. The solicitor was reading Humphrey's will and had just come to the last paragraph. 'I always said I'd mention my dear wife, Joan, in my will,' read out the solicitor. 'So, hello there, Joan!'

976. Paul's grandmother changed her Will six times – she was a fresh heir fiend.

WISHES
977. A little old lady was busy making herself some tea one afternoon when a fairy appeared in her kitchen.

'You've led a long and good life,' said the fairy, 'so I've come to reward you and tell you that you can make three wishes. Ask for absolutely anything you like and with one wave of my magic wand; you can have it.'

The old lady found this very difficult to believe, so she asked the fairy to turn the teapot into lots of lovely money.

The fairy waved her magic wand and the teapot promptly turned into a pile of money.

'My!' exclaimed the old lady. 'It really does work! Now, can you make me look young and beautiful?'

The fairy waved her wand again and in a few seconds the little old lady was transformed into someone looking young and beautiful.

'And now I'd like you to turn my dear old cat into a handsome, young man.'

This, too, was soon done, and the fairy left the old-but-now-young-and-beautiful-looking-lady alone in her kitchen with the handsome young man who had formerly been a cat.

The lady turned to the man and sighed: 'At last! Now I want to make love to you for the rest of the day and night!'

The man looked at her, then said, in a very high pitched voice: 'Then you shouldn't have taken me to the vet's, should you?'

WITCHES
978. Why do witches fly around on broomsticks?
Because vacuum cleaners are too noisy.

WOODPECKERS
979. A woodpecker was talking to a chicken. 'Woodpeckers are much cleverer than you chickens.'

'What makes you say that?' asked the chicken. 'You seem to spend all your day banging your head against a tree.'

'Ah!' responded the woodpecker. 'But have you ever heard of Kentucky Fried Woodpecker?'

WORK
980. Mr Williams was angry with his son, who just seemed to laze about the house all day, even though he had been given a good education and was now twenty-two years old.

'You can't hang around waiting for a top job to come along,' said Mr Williams. 'You've got to start somewhere. Why don't you do the same as I did? Start as a humble accounts clerk. Within five years I'd made enough to start my own business.'

'I know Dad,' replied the son, 'but that's not possible these days – they have proper auditors now!'

X

X-RAY

981. The medical lecturer in the newly opened Medical School turned to one of his pupils and said: 'Now, Jones, it is clear from this X-Ray I am holding up that one of this patient's legs is considerably shorter than the other. This of course, accounts for the patient's limp. But what would *you* do in a case like this?'

Jones thought for a few seconds, then said, brightly: 'I should imagine, sir, that I would limp, too.'

Y

YEAST

982. A friend of mine eats yeast and shoe polish before going to bed – he likes to rise and shine.

Z

ZEBRA CROSSING
983. Policeman to jay-walking pedestrian: 'Here! Why are you crossing the road in this dangerous spot – can't you see there's a zebra crossing only fifty yards away?'

Pedestrian: 'Well, I hope it's having better luck than I am.'

ZOO
984. The little boy had just returned home after an outing with his father.

'Well, dear, how did you like the zoo?' asked the boy's mother.

'Oh, it was great!' replied the boy. 'And Dad liked it too – especially when one of the animals came racing home at thirty to one.'

985. I hear that at the local zoo they are trying to cross a carrier pigeon with a woodpecker: they are aiming to breed a bird that will not only deliver messages but also knock first.

Also available from
Elliot Right Way Books

THE PUBLIC SPEAKER'S JOKE BOOK

Another collection of jokes, compiled by Kevin Goldstein-Jackson, which is ideal for the public speaker (or for a hilarious read on a plane or train journey or for a chuckle in bed). The jokes suit every occasion: business functions, conventions, dinners, weddings and children's parties, so you'll never be lost for a humorous quip.

YOUR VOICE
How to Enrich it, and Develop it for Speaking, Acting and Everyday Conversation

A simple but valuable guide for those who want to polish and improve their most potent means of communication: the voice. Become aware of the parts of your body which need to work to peak performance for clear, dynamic and persuasive speech. Be guided through the use of crisp consonants and well shaped vowels. Learn expressiveness, projection, confidence and relaxation.

WEDDING SPEECHES

This book consists entirely of wedding speeches. There are 15 speeches for the bridegroom, 15 for the best man, 12 for the bride's father (along with another 8 suitable for occasions when the bride's father does not speak), and 15 which are suitable for other relations and friends who may want to say something.

RIGHT WAY
PUBLISHING POLICY

HOW WE SELECT TITLES

RIGHT WAY consider carefully every deserving manuscript. Where an author is an authority on his subject but an inexperienced writer, we provide first-class editorial help. The standards we set make sure that every **RIGHT WAY** book is practical, easy to understand, concise, informative and delightful to read. Our specialist artists are skilled at creating simple illustrations which augment the text wherever necessary.

CONSISTENT QUALITY

At every reprint our books are updated where appropriate, giving our authors the opportunity to include new information.

FAST DELIVERY

We sell **RIGHT WAY** books to the best bookshops throughout the world. It may be that your bookseller has run out of stock of a particular title. If so, he can order more from us at any time – we have a fine reputation for "same day" despatch, and we supply any order, however small (even a single copy), to any bookseller who has an account with us. We prefer you to buy from your bookseller, as this reminds him of the strong underlying public demand for **RIGHT WAY** books. Readers who live in remote places, or who are housebound, or whose local bookseller is uncooperative, can order direct from us by post.

FREE

If you would like an up-to-date list of all **RIGHT WAY** titles currently available, please send a stamped self-addressed envelope to

ELLIOT RIGHT WAY BOOKS,
KINGSWOOD, SURREY, KT20 6TD, U.K.
or visit our web site at www.right-way.co.uk